KEY SKILLS
IN A LEVEL ENGLISH

JANE BLUETT & PIP FLEWITT

Hodder & Stoughton
A MEMBER OF THE HODDER HEADLINE GROUP

820.9

Acknowledgement
Cover: emma@Redseal

The publishers would like to thank the following for permission to reproduce copyright material:

Text permissions: pp 30–33 'Nokia nk402 Instruction Book' © Orange Mobile Phones; pp 58–63 'London Marathon booklet' © Whizz-Kidz; p 65–6, 'Flora London Marathon 2000 Offical Programme' © The London Marathon Ltd.; pp 77–8 *Soulmates* © The Guardian; pp 91–3 Metropolitan Journal March, 1993 © Metropolitan Police; pp 94–5 © Victims Support 1991/92 Annual Report; pp 102–3 © The Independent/ Syndication; pp 104–5 *Talking from 9 to 5* © Deborah Tannen, Virago Press.

Artwork permissions: p 30 © Secol; pp 31–2, 58 © Perception Design; pp 59, 60, 62 © Bartholomew Ltd. 2001. Reproduced by Permission of Harper Collins Publishers; p 63, The London Marathon Ltd.; pp 82–3 Caroline Parkinson from High Pavement College.

Every effort has been made to trace copyright holders of material reproduced in this book. Any rights not acknowledged will be acknowledged in subsequent printings it notice is given to the publisher.

Orders: please contact Bookpoint Ltd, 130 Milton Park, Abingdon, Oxon OX14 4SB. Telephone: (44) 01235 827720, Fax: (44) 01235 400454. Lines are open from 9.00–6.00, Monday to Saturday, with a 24 hour message answering service. Email address: orders@bookpoint.co.uk

British Library Cataloguing in Publication Data
A catalogue record for this title is available from The British Library

ISBN 0 340 80202 2

First published 2001
Impression number   10 9 8 7 6 5 4 3 2 1
Year   2007 2006 2005 2004 2003 2002 2001

Copyright © 2001 Pip Flewitt and Jane Bluett

Typeset by Fakenham Photosetting Ltd., Fakenham, Norfolk.
Printed in Great Britain for Hodder & Stoughton Educational, a division of Hodder Headline Plc, 338 Euston Road, London NW1 3BH by Hobbs the Printers Ltd., Totton, Hampshire.

CONTENTS

INTRODUCTION

We all know that one of the main purposes of English teaching is to facilitate communication. Now that there is a formal qualification in Key Skills Communication it gives A Level English students the chance to gain extra credit for the work that they do as part of their courses. The purpose of this book is to show how current practice in A Level English teaching can be adapted to target specifically the demands of the new qualification.

The activities in this book have been designed to fit in with existing syllabus structures as we believe that the whole point of Key Skills is to enhance the student's experience of English without increasing the student's or the teacher's workload.

It is not necessary to be an English teacher, or to be an A Level English student, to use the activities within this book. Many of the activities can be used for the general provision of Communication Key Skills at Level 3.

The first set of differentiated exercises is designed to encourage speaking and listening. They target **C3.1a** and **C3.1b** but they will not earn a key skills award by themselves. You will need to progress to the second set of exercises when you feel ready to tackle the testing element of the course.

The exercises in this book will help you to develop your skills of:

- Effective listening

- Dealing with complex subjects

- Contributing to discussions

- Making a presentation.

You can choose whether to try one or two of the exercises in order to strengthen one particular skill or if you prefer, you can build them all into a scheme of work.

All support materials have been provided for you.

The final section of the book contains two exemplar tests complete with reference material and marking guidelines.

DRAW A SHAPE

This introductory task enables students to work towards achieving Level 3 Key Skill in Communication.

AIM

To encourage precise and attentive listening.

EQUIPMENT NEEDED

Rough paper and pens

GROUPING

Groups of three

TIME

One lesson

TASK

Two students (A and B) have one minute to draw a shape on a piece of paper without letting anyone else see the shape. The third student (C) acts as an observer and times the exercise.

Students A and B sit back to back. Student A describes the shape they have drawn and student B draws this from A's verbal description. They have one minute to do this and are timed by C. The students then swap roles.

When both shapes have been redrawn, the pictures are compared with the originals. The students should then all discuss why differences have occurred and list strategies for making descriptions clearer and less ambiguous next time, for example they should start with simple shapes, use squared paper and so on.

The exercise is then repeated twice, rotating the roles so each student acts as an observer once and participant twice.

STICKLEBRICK EXERCISE

This introductory task allows students to work towards achieving Level 3 Key Skill in Communication.

AIMS

To develop reporting skills.

To develop observation skills.

To encourage listening skills.

To develop team building skills.

To develop a precise questioning technique.

EQUIPMENT NEEDED

Four or five containers, containing exactly the same number, shape and colour of Sticklebricks or Lego bricks or similar construction equipment. (Not provided.)

One copy of Group Roles sheet per group.

GROUPING

Groups of four or five are ideal but the exercise can be done with larger groups.

TIME

One lesson.

TASK

Before the start of this activity the teacher will need to create a shape from Sticklebricks or from Lego. The shape should not resemble a house or a vehicle as this will make it too easy to describe. Try to create a challenging but memorable shape which can be communicated to the group members.

The aim of the exercise is for the students to simulate the roles of architect, foreman and builders and to recreate a structure. The group has to assess the strengths and weaknesses of its members and assign roles. The teacher's role is to build the original structure using about 20 to 25 Sticklebricks of different shapes, sizes and colours. The structure should then be placed out of sight, preferably out of the classroom, and covered up. The teacher will then need to prepare identical packs of Sticklebricks so that the shape can be recreated by the group. The teacher will need to prepare as many packs of bricks as there are groups. Each pack has to contain exactly the same bricks as the original structure.

ACTIVITY

The activity begins when the group has allocated roles to its members. The teacher gives the pack of Sticklebricks to the builders and asks all the architects to leave the room.

The architects will now be allowed to study the structure made of Sticklebricks that has been placed conveniently outside the classroom. The architects will be allowed to see the model for exactly three minutes. The architects are not allowed to take any notes whilst they are looking at the building so all the architects will need to have a good memory.

After three minutes, the model will be covered up and the architects will be allowed to meet with the foremen. The builders will not be allowed to listen to the conversation. The foremen will be able to ask questions and make notes on anything the architects say BUT the architects can not write or draw anything for the foremen. The only medium for communication at this stage must be word of mouth. Architects can talk to the foremen for three minutes. The foremen will then rejoin the builders. The architects must not have any communication with the builders.

It is the job of the foremen to instruct the builders to build the model which the architect has explained to them. The foremen cannot touch the Sticklebricks. All communication between foremen and builders must be verbal. The builders will not have access to the foreman's notes. IMPORTANT – the foremen can request two more meetings with the architect if they need extra information.

The task is for the builders to build the model that only the architect has seen. The success of the building depends on the effectiveness of the communication within the group.

STICKLEBRICK EXERCISE

STUDENT SHEET

Group Roles

Look at the definitions of the following roles and decide which members of your group are best suited to these roles. You need to make your decisions quickly as you only have three minutes to sort yourselves out.

Architect

You need to have a good memory and be able to give clear, concise instructions. People need to trust you. You need to be accurate and decisive. You have to give a clear lead.

Foremen (1 or 2 depending on group size)

You need to be good at liaising with people. You need to be able to listen and ask appropriate questions. You need to be able to take careful notes, which you can then explain to the other members of your group. You are a go-between, and the success of the building largely depends on you.

Builders (2–4)

You need to be able to listen and understand instructions. You need to be able to ask questions which clarify the instructions you have been given. You need to be able to act on the instructions you have been given without changing them in any way. You are part of a team which requires you to carry out instructions exactly.

KIDNEY MACHINE

This introductory task allows students to work towards Level 3 Key Skills in Communication or to achieve Level 2.

AIMS

To develop skills in argument and persuasion.

To develop skills in reaching a consensus.

To develop decision making skills.

To learn to change or adapt decisions in the light of new information.

EQUIPMENT NEEDED

Copies of Sheet 1 The Patients

Copies of Sheet 2 Additional Information

Copies of Sheet 3 Preferences

GROUPING

Groups of 4–6

TIME

Decide who lives – 1 hour

Preferences – 30 minutes

Kidney Machine

TASK 1

Divide the class into groups. Each group will be role-playing a team of doctors with limited funds. The doctors have met to discuss an important problem. Within their practice there are SIX patients who have been diagnosed as having kidney failure. These patients are now very seriously ill and need dialysis on a regular basis.

Each patient requires the sole use of a kidney dialysis machine. Unfortunately, due to shortages of funds, there are only TWO dialysis machines available. The patients who are lucky enough to have a dialysis machine will probably get a kidney transplant at a later date. All six patients have a life expectance of three weeks without artificial dialysis.

Issue **Sheet 1** to each group. Do not tell them that there is any additional information. Ask each group to decide which two patients will be offered kidney machines. Every member of the group must agree on the decision. The group will then be asked to justify their decision to the whole class.

Issue **Sheet 2**. This gives additional information about the patients. The group might want to change their decisions in the light of this new information. Allow time for the group to discuss any possible changes and reach a consensus. Once again, each group has to justify their decisions and any changes in their earlier decisions to the whole class. Allow a different group member to report back to the whole class.

Optional Extension Activity

It is probable that each group will have made different choices. You might want to extend the discussion process to see if the whole class can reach a consensus on which two patients will have the machines, and of course, the chance of life.

TASK 2

MERTHYR TYDFIL COLLEGE
LIBRARY

Give each group **Sheet 3**. This list of patients was compiled by a newspaper and was distributed to GPs. The GPs were asked to rank the patients in the order that they felt merited being offered a kidney machine. The newspaper used the data from the GPs who responded to compile a national list.

Ask the students to discuss the criteria which might be used by doctors to differentiate between kidney patients, for example if a patient was suffering from another life threatening disease would they be a high priority for a kidney machine? If a patient was unlikely to be disciplined enough to carry out the prescribed treatment effectively, would they be a high or low priority for a kidney machine? When the students have explored possible criteria that might affect their decisions, ask them to look at the list of patients on sheet 3. They have to decide on a rank order of preference, putting patients who would automatically be given a machine at the top of the list.

(Note: You might prefer to cut up the sheet into individual names as this makes it easier to rearrange.)

The GPs actual preferred list is on **Sheet 4**. You might like to discuss this with the students at the end of the activity.

KIDNEY MACHINE

⫽ SHEET 1: THE PATIENTS

SIX patients suffering from kidney failure.

TWO kidney machines.

The people who are offered kidney machines will probably get a kidney transplant at a later date.

The FOUR people who do not receive dialysis will die within three weeks.

The Patients

KAREL MATEK	Nobel philosopher	aged 58 years	married – no children
JANE SMITH	Shop Assistant	aged 19 years	single – no children
ALEXANDER FULLERTON	Public schoolboy	aged 17 years	single – no children
BILL FRANKS	Factory worker	aged 32 years	married – 3 children two aged 5, 1 aged 7
MAGGIE JONES	Housewife	aged 42 years	married – 2 children aged 21 and 23
OBO NGAME	Doctor	aged 32 years	married – 1 child aged 8 years

Choose TWO patients to go on to the kidney machines.

SHEET 2: ADDITIONAL INFORMATION

Karel Matek
Origin – Hungary. Naturalised British in 1955. Age 58
Professor of Philosophy at Oxford University
Nobel prize for peace
Married – no children
Wife, Jean is a district nurse.
Religion – Catholic
Previous medical history – Good. Kidney failure probably due to treatment by the Gestapo (NAZI security police) in WW2.
I.Q. 160 plus

Jane Smith
English. Age 19
Shop Assistant
Single – no children
Religion – nominally Church of England
Previous medical history – Jaundice (severe), T.B.
I.Q. 90

Alexander Fullerton
English. Age 17
Attends Eton Public School
Has passed open examination to Kings College, Cambridge
Single – no children
Religion – Quaker
Previous medical history – deformed by Thalidomide during mother's pregnancy (one arm and two legs). He is sterile and his kidney failure is due to the Thalidomide.
I.Q. 160 plus

Bill Franks
English. Age 32
Factory worker (toolmaker), Town Councillor
Married. Wife aged 30 years, housewife.
Three children. Two boys aged 5 and 7, girl aged 5.
Religion – Methodist
Previous medical history – appendicitis and broken leg (football).
I.Q. 120

Maggie Jones
English. Age 42
Housewife
Married. Husband is a company director.
Two children. Girls aged 21 and 23, both married.
Religion – Church of England
Previous medical history – 2 pregnancies, varicose veins and incipient arthritis.
I.Q. 108

Obo Ngame
Burmese. Age 32
Doctor
Married. Wife, Gillian, also a doctor.
One child aged 8.
Religion – Buddhist
Previous medical history – Malaria.
I.Q. 135

SHEET 3: PREFERENCES

Put these patients into the order which you would offer kidney treatment.

51 year old woman with breast cancer

53 year old male diabetic

59 year old female diabetic

55 year old woman with asthma

50 year old man with ischaemic heart disease

62 year old man recovering from stroke

72 year old male vet

50 year old educationally subnormal woman

30 year old man with schizophrenia

29 year old hepatitis B positive man

52 year old male alcoholic

25 year old blind male diabetic

45 year old female analgesic abuser

38 year old man with paraplegia

49 year old woman with rheumatoid arthritis

67 year old Asian with no English

SHEET 4: GPS PREFERRED LIST

In the queue for kidney treatment, this was the list, in order of preference, chosen by specialists and printed in the British Medical Journal.

55 year old woman with asthma

72 year old male vet

38 year old man with paraplegia

53 year old male diabetic

59 year old female diabetic

25 year old blind male diabetic

62 year old man recovering from stroke

49 year old woman with rheumatoid arthritis

50 year old educationally subnormal woman

45 year old female analgesic abuser

67 year old Asian with no English

51 year old woman with breast cancer

50 year old man with ischaemic heart disease

30 year old man with schizophrenia

52 year old male alcoholic

29 year old hepatitis B positive man

HAIRDRESSERS

A hugely enjoyable task that allows students to develop their oral communication skills, teamwork, role-play and problem solving skills.

AIM

To develop team building skills.

To develop communication skills.

EQUIPMENT NEEDED

One copy of the Judge Sheet

One copy of the Team Instruction Sheet per team

One copy of the Observer's Sheet

Bits of Information Sheet, 1 per student

GROUPING

Teams of six to eight

TIME

One lesson

TASK

Students should work in teams of six to eight. Each team member (A–F) is given a Bits of Information Sheet. One member of the team should take charge of the instructions. Any extra team members can be appointed observers.

It is the team's task to find out:

a)   Who is going on holiday.

b)   Who is having a restyle.

Teams should be allowed to work the task out for themselves. The teacher should be the Judge and hold the solution sheet. A student could be the Judge if class size permits.

Team presentations of their experience should be made to the rest of the class at the end of the exercise.

All the information needed is contained in the following pages.

HAIRDRESSERS

JUDGE SHEET

1. Your job is to enforce the rules and judge the team's solution.

2. Study carefully the Hairdressers Team Instruction Sheet. Ask the team members if they have read and understood their instructions. Answer any questions before they begin work.

3. When the team is ready, give each member a different copy of the Hairdressers Bits of Information Sheet, (A–F), and tell the members to begin working. Record their start time.

4. Enforce the rules, for example, do not allow the team members to write anything.

5. If the team tells you that the task has been completed, check whether or not the answers are correct:
   a) *Martha is going on holiday.*
   b) *Barbara is having the restyle.*

6. If the answers are correct, record the time at which the team finished the task, and report to the facilitator that the team has finished.

7. If only one of the above answers is given to you, or if the group begins to recite additional answers not asked for – such as 'Martha is going on holiday and Evelyn's hairdresser is Paul', announce that the task is incomplete. Instruct the members to keep on working until they finish one required task or until the facilitator stops the activity.

Solution

Customer	Barbara	Delia	Evelyn	Jenny	Martha
Dog	Poodle	Labrador	Cairn Terrier	Bull Dog	Red Setter
Town	Bongleton	Munchfield	Looncester	Hardingly	Bagnal Parva
Hairdresser	Tony	Samantha	Paul	Julie	Liz
Style	Restyle*	Colour Rinse	Blow-dry	Highlights	Perm
Event	Birthday Party	Theatre Visit	Wedding Anniversary	Lunch Engagement	Holiday*

* Items to be deduced by the team

HAIRDRESSERS

TEAM INSTRUCTION SHEET

1. Your group's judge will tell you when and how to start working.

2. Each member of the team will receive written bits of information. These are not to be shown to others.

3. What will be required of you, and how to go about it, will become clear as you share information with the other members of your team, through verbal communication only.

4. When you and your co-workers feel that the required tasks have been completed, call the judge to check your results.

5. If your tasks have been only partially completed, or if you have done more than what was required, the judge will consider the tasks as being totally incomplete. In that case you will be required to keep on working without the benefit of knowing which part of your task, if any, has been completed satisfactorily.

6. The following rules will be observed throughout this activity:
    a) From the moment the team begins work, members may speak to other team members only.
    b) You may not show others the contents of your written bits of information.
    c) You may not write anything.
    d) You must obey the judge's instructions.

7. You will have sixty minutes in which to complete your task.

HAIRDRESSERS

OBSERVER'S SHEET

1. Your job is to observe your team's progress, record it and report your observations to the entire team.

2. Do not reach conclusions or attribute intentions and feelings to others. Simply describe what you actually see.

3. Read the Hairdressers Team Instruction Sheet in order to familiarise yourself with the task and the ground rules.
   The team is given bits of information from which it is to determine who is having a restyle and who going on holiday.

4. Use the following guide, add whatever seems pertinent and consult the solution table as an aid for your observations.

Individual Analysis

a) Who initiates action, how is it done and what is the action?

b) Who contributes to or obstructs the task? How? Is the behaviour effective?

c) How is the leadership issue managed.

Group Analysis

a) Did the members know and agree on the required tasks prior to the problem solving, or did they start working immediately?

b) What patterns of communications developed?

c) What procedures to solve the problem developed?

d) How was the data gathered and compiled?

e) What was the climate that emerged? Were there any turning points?

f) Other.

Cut out the Bits of Information Sheets and hand out to each member of the team.

ANALYSING COMMUNICATION

Hairdressers – Bits of Information
Sheet A

- The woman who is having a perm also has a Red Setter.
- The woman who is going to the birthday party lives in Bongleton.
- The Bull Dog's owner who is going to a lunch engagement is having her hair styled by Julie.
- Tony is not giving his client a blow-dry.
- Each of the customers has a different breed of dog.
- Barbara is getting ready for a birthday party.

Hairdressers – Bits of Information
Sheet B

- The woman who lives in Bagnal Parva is not going to the theatre.
- Your group has less than three tasks.
- Paul is attending to the woman's hair who lives in Looncester.
- Delia is not telling her stylist about a wedding anniversary.
- Evelyn is having her hair styled by a man.

Hairdressers – Bits of Information
Sheet C

- Delia and Martha are not going to the birthday party.
- The owner of the Cairn Terrier is not having a restyle.
- The Red Setter will go into kennels while its owner goes on holiday.
- The woman who is having the blow-dry is making plans to celebrate the coming wedding anniversary.
- Martha does not own the Poodle.
- Liz is not giving her client a colour rinse.

Hairdressers – Bits of Information
Sheet D

- Julie is painfully pulling strands of hair through a plastic cap in order to give her client the required highlights.
- One of your group's tasks is to decide who is having a restyle.
- The Labrador's owner is having a colour rinse.
- Jenny is telling her stylist all about the lunch engagement the next day.

Hairdressers – Bits of Information
Sheet E

- The woman who is giving her client a perm is not Samantha.
- Evelyn is the owner of the Cairn Terrier.
- The Labrador's owner lives in Munchfield.
- The woman who owns the Poodle is going to a birthday party.
- The Bull Dog's owner lives in Hardingly.
- The woman who is going on holiday is not having her hair styled by a man.

Hairdressers – Bits of Information
Sheet F

- Tony is hearing all about the birthday party that is to take place in the evening.
- The owner of the Cairn Terrier lives at Looncester.
- Delia lives in Munchfield.
- One of your group's tasks is to decide who is going on holiday.
- The woman who is having highlights lives in Hardingly.

SKILLS

What makes people effective communicators and exactly what is effective communication? One of the reasons you are reading this is because you are working towards a Key Skills qualification in Communication. It will help you if you spend a little time analysing how people communicate effectively because it will help you to develop these skills.

If you are listening to a discussion or if you are acting as an observer for any of these oral exercises you need to be able to answer the following questions.

1. In the discussion you have observed or been a part of:
   a) Who contributed willingly?
   b) Who had to be invited to speak?
   c) Who dominated the discussion?
   d) Who seemed to you the most effective communicator?

2. When the group was asked to consider new ideas:
   a) Who offered new ideas?
   b) Who responded to these ideas with further ideas of their own?
   c) Who was unable to move away from their own idea even if it was found to be unsuitable?

3. Do people actually listen to each other? Did you notice:
   a) Were points answered or were they merely stated?
   b) Did speakers pick up on the points made by others or did they just continue with their own line of argument?
   c) Was there more talking than listening?
   d) If a person is not speaking, is it safe to assume that they are listening?

4. What is the difference between a discussion and an argument?

How would you assess your own communication skills if you had to observe yourself?

CAVE RESCUE

dents to achieve **C3.1a**. It could also be used as the basis for a
ther extended writing activities that would allow students to
nents of the Key Skills qualification.

....

explore complex moral and ethical issues.

skills.

guement and persuasion.

....

D

ng Sheet per group and a copy of the Volunteer Personal
udent.

....

ple.

....

ng a long time to complete you can use the following
move things along:

He offers great wealth to ensure her rescue.

News Flash

Paul's treatment has just been recognised as a possible cure for HIV.

News Flash

The water is rising faster than you thought. At least two people will die.

Always remind the students that whatever solution has been agreed by the group
and is committed to by every member of the group is the RIGHT answer.

CAVE RESCUE BRIEFING SHEET

Your group is asked to take the role of a research management committee who are funding projects into human behaviour in confined spaces.

You have been called to an emergency meeting as one of the experiments has gone badly wrong.

Six volunteers have been taken into a cave system in a remote part of the country, connected only by a radio link to the research hut by the cave entrance. It was intended that the volunteers would spend four days underground, but they have been trapped by falling rocks and rising water.

The only rescue team available tells you that rescue will be extremely difficult and only one person can be brought out each hour with the equipment at their disposal. It is likely that the rapidly rising water will drown some of the volunteers before rescue can be effected.

The volunteers are aware of the dangers of their plight. They have contacted the research hut using the radio link and said that they are unwilling to take a decision as to the sequence by which they will be rescued. By the terms of the research project, the responsibility for making this decision now rests with your committee.

Life saving equipment will arrive in 50 minutes at the cave entrance and you will need to advise the team of the order for rescue by completing the ranking sheet.

The only information you have available is drawn from the project files and is reproduced on the volunteer personal detail sheet. You may use any criteria you think fit to help you make a decision.

Ranking Sheet

Order of Rescue	Name

VOLUNTEER PERSONAL DETAIL SHEET

Volunteer 1: Helen

Helen is 34 years old and a housewife. She has four children aged between 7 months and 8 years. Her hobbies are ice-skating and cooking. She lives in a pleasant house in Gloucester, and was born in England. Helen is known to have developed a covert romantic and sexual relationship with another volunteer (Owen).

Volunteer 2: Tozo

Tozo is 19 years old and a sociology student at Keele University. She is the daughter of wealthy Japanese parents who live in Tokyo. Her father is an industrialist who is also a national authority on traditional Japanese mime theatre. Tozo is unmarried but has several highborn suitors, as she is outstandingly attractive. She has recently been the subject of a TV documentary on Japanese womanhood and flower arranging.

Volunteer 3: Jobe

Jobe is a man of 41 years and was born in Central Africa. He is a minister of religion whose life work has been devoted to the social and political evolution of African peoples. Jobe is a member of the Communist Party and has paid several visits to the USSR in recent years. He is married with eleven children whose ages range from 6 years to 19 years. His hobby is playing in a jazz band.

Volunteer 4: Owen

Owen is an unmarried man of 27 years. As a short-commission officer he spent part of his service in Northern Ireland where, as an undercover agent, he broke up an IRA cell and received a special commendation in dispatches. Since returning to civilian life he has been unsettled and drinking has become a persistent problem. At present he is a Youth Adventure Leader, devoting much energy to helping young people and leading caving groups. His recreation is preparing and driving stock cars. He lives in Brecon, South Wales.

Volunteer 5: Paul

Paul is a man of 42 who has been divorced for six years. His ex-wife is now happily re-married. He was born in Scotland, but now lives in Richmond, Surrey. Paul works as a medical research scientist at the Hammersmith Hospital and he is recognized as a world authority on the treatment of rabies. He has recently developed a low-cost treatment that could be self-administered. Much of the research data is still in his work notebooks. Unfortunately, Paul has experienced some emotional difficulties in recent years and has twice been convicted of indecent exposure. The last occasion was 11 months ago. His hobbies are classical music, opera and sailing.

Volunteer 6: Edward

Edward is a man of 59 years who has lived and worked in Barnsley for most of his life. He is general manager of a factory producing rubber belts for machines. The factory employs 71 persons. He is prominent in local society; and is a Freemason and a Conservative Councillor. He is married with two children who have their own families and have moved away from Barnsley. Edward has recently returned from Poland where he was personally responsible for promoting a contract to supply large numbers of industrial belts over a five-year period. This contract, if signed, would mean work for another 26 people. Edward's hobbies include collecting antique guns, and he intends to write a book about Civil War Armaments on his retirement. He is also a strong cricket supporter.

FORMAL DEBATE

This task addresses Key Skill C3.1a.

AIM
To introduce students to the language, experience and possibilities of a formal debate and allow them to adopt the role of expert.

EQUIPMENT NEEDED
One copy of the pupil sheets (How to Organise a Formal Debate) per group.

GROUPING
Groups of five and the whole class at different stages.

TIME
One session to prepare the debate.
Two or more sessions to hear all the debates. The exact time will depend on how much argument is put forward.

TASK

Explain the general principle of debating and discuss the formal roles which have to be taken. Discuss possible topics for debate. These might include 'This house holds that this college should cease to be a Non Smoking College', 'This house holds that women are more intelligent than men', 'This house holds that men are better drivers than women', 'This house holds that a woman's place is in the home', 'This house holds that recreational drugs should be legalised'. The class will probably want to choose their own topics.

Divide the class into groups of five. Issue the pupil sheets How to Organise a Formal Debate, to each group of students. Each group can elect a chairperson and fill all the other roles. The remainder of the lesson is spent preparing the individual speeches for the debate.

Next lesson, hear the debates.

HOW TO ORGANISE A FORMAL DEBATE

A debate is a formal discussion where speakers try to persuade the audience to agree with their point of view. All debates begin with a **motion** or statement of opinion. The motion is expressed in the following words

This house holds that . . .

An example of a motion for debate is:

This house holds that women are better drivers than men.

The motion needs to be **proposed** and **opposed**.

The **proposer** is the person who speaks first and explains to the audience why the idea is a good one and why he or she feels that the house or audience need to support it.

The **opposer** is the second person to speak. Their job is to disagree totally with the motion and they tell the house exactly why they cannot agree with the point of view put forward by the proposer. They will try to persuade the audience to disagree with the motion.

The next person to speak is the **seconder for the motion**. They have quite a difficult job because not only will they have prepared some ideas themselves in support of the motion, but they will also have to think on their feet and try to discuss ideas put forward by the first two speakers. Their job is to give additional support to the proposer's ideas and at the same time, find fault with the opposer's ideas.

The final speaker is the **seconder against the motion**. Like the seconder for the motion they have to support the opposer but they need to have listened carefully to all three speakers so that they can point out the flaws in the proposer's arguments whilst giving additional support to the opposition. This role calls for a very confident speaker.

The **chairperson** is the one to whom all these speeches are addressed. If the audience want to ask the speakers any questions, these too are addressed to the chairperson.

The chairperson has a clearly defined role to play. It is their job to explain all the procedures of the debate to the audience so that the audience knows exactly what is going to happen. They will introduce the speakers and explain the topic to be debated.

It is also useful to have a **timekeeper** who makes sure each speaker has the same amount of time.

SEATING PLAN

All four speakers and the chairperson need to sit at the front of the room. They could sit behind a table with the chairperson in the middle, the two speakers proposing the motion on his or her right and the speakers opposing the motion on his or her left.

THE DEBATE

Before the debate can begin, the chairperson has to set a time limit for each speaker, usually about six minutes. The speakers cannot go over their time limit. The timekeeper will be responsible for making sure no one has more than their allotted time.

The chairperson tells the audience what topic is being debated and explains the order of events. They then introduce the speakers and read out the motion for debate.

The proposer is addressed by name and asked to speak for the motion. The proposer then speaks for the agreed time.

The chairperson then turns to the opposer and addressing them by their name, asks them to speak against the motion. The opposer then speaks. Now it is the turn of the seconders. They usually have half the time limit allocated to the first speakers, in this case they will speak for three minutes.

The chairperson will invite the seconder for the motion to speak. They will add some new points of their own but they will take any opportunity they can of dismissing the argument put forward by the opposition. (You have perhaps seen this done by politicians.) The seconder's job is to get the audience to support them by making the opposition look foolish.

The chairperson now invites the seconder against the motion to speak. As before, they will try to make the arguments put forward by the proposer look foolish. They often use rhetorical questions which do not require any answer but which play on the emotions of the listeners.

Now that the speakers have had their turn, it is time for the audience to get involved. The chairperson will invite members of the audience to ask questions or make comments about what they have heard. The audience is referred to as the floor of the house. The questions are always addressed to the chairperson and it is their job to pass on the question to one of the speakers. They might even repeat the question in their own words. This is called restating it. Sometimes this part of the debate can become quite heated and it is the chairperson's job to maintain order.

When there are no more questions we move on to the final section of the debate, the summing up. The chairperson will ask the proposer to sum up their point of view. They will have to keep to a time limit of two or three minutes.

The proposer will use this time to remind the house why they should support their motion. The speaker needs to play on the audience's emotions here.

The chairperson then invites the opposer to sum up and they too will make an impassioned plea for the house to support their opposition to the motion. They must keep to the same time limit as the proposer. It is the timekeeper's job to make sure this is so.

The chairperson now puts the motion. The motion is read out to the floor and the audience is asked to vote. The people who agree with the motion are the ayes and the people who disagree are the noes. the chairperson asks for a show of hands for the ayes and then a show of hands for the noes. A teller is appointed to count these and hand the result to the chairperson. The chairperson announces the result and states that 'The motion is carried' or 'The motion is lost'.

The house then applauds.

TEN TOP TIPS

1. Choose your speakers carefully. The proposer and opposer can work from a prepared script but the seconders need to have the ability to react to what the other speakers are saying.

2. Make sure the speakers have pen and paper handy to note down ideas from the opposition so that they can attack them.

3. When you stand up to speak, look confident and sincere.

4. Try not to look as if you are reading from a script – even if you are!

5. Use cue cards as prompts.

6. You are allowed to be amusing but you are not allowed to be insulting. Be careful what you say about the other speakers.

7. Try to get the audience on your side.

8. Do not say anything you cannot prove.

9. Plant questions in the audience. You can have the answers already prepared in advance.

10. Make sure you finish on your best point.

GIVING A TALK

This task allows students to earn Key Skill C3.1b.

AIMS

To encourage students to structure information clearly using an image. To encourage the development of drafting skills and to develop confidence in presenting themselves.

EQUIPMENT NEEDED

One copy of the Giving a Talk pupil sheet.

GROUPING

Groups of four.

TIME

One hour to prepare the talk.

30 minutes to hear the talks.

TASK

Ask each student to prepare a three minute talk on any topic using the Giving a Talk pupil sheet provided. Discuss how to make notes for a talk and how to use key facts as prompts. The students must use an image of some kind, a picture, a poster, a photograph, a drawing or an OHP transparency. The talk cannot be fully scripted.

Ask the students to join together with their friends to form a group of four. The aim is for each student to deliver his or her talk to that group. Giving a talk is a frightening prospect for most people. We hope that by making this a small group activity rather than a speech in front of the whole class, students will find the prospect less daunting.

Note: A selection of topics relating to the A Level English syllabuses can be found towards the end of this book.

The teacher might prefer to have more than one group working simultaneously. This saves time and is more comfortable for students. A good way of evidencing this activity would be to use a video recorder or a cassette tape.

GIVING A TALK

STRUCTURING A TALK

If you are not sure exactly how to give a talk you might like to follow these guidelines.

1 Introduction

Tell your audience what you are going to be talking about and break your topic down into four or five main areas. List these, saying: These are the main points of my talk.

2 Opening point

Your opening point needs to gain the attention of the audience so try to think of an interesting way of introducing your idea. Try to give an example to help the audience understand your point of view. Develop your idea and then prepare to link it to your second point.

3 Second point

Make sure the ideas you are talking about follow on logically from each other. develop your second idea, giving examples where possible and link this to your third point.

4 Third point, Fourth point and Fifth point

Continue through your ideas in the order you introduced them to the audience.

5 Concluding comments

Summarise the main issues of your talk and end with a well considered final remark. Your audience will remember your closing sentence more than your opening sentence so it is worthwhile spending a little time planning a good ending.

MOBILE PHONE

This task allows students to earn Key Skill C3.1a and C3.1b.

AIM

To encourage precise and clear transmission of information.

EQUIPMENT NEEDED

Two copies of the labelled drawing of the mobile phone and one copy of the operating instructions per group. A tape recorder might also be useful.

GROUPING

In twos or threes

TIME

One hour

TASK

Student A has bought a second hand mobile phone from a friend but the operating manual has been lost. Student A knows that Student B has a similar mobile phone and telephones them to find out how to use the phone she has just bought.

Students A and B sit back to back. Both have a copy of the diagram of the phone but only student B has a copy of the operating instructions. Pupil C is an observer. A questions B about how to use the phone. She wants to know how to charge the battery, how to make a call, how to answer a call, and how to send a text message. Student B might decide to offer additional information about the screen symbols.

At the end of the exercise the students discuss how effective the transmission of information has been and how they could improve it.

The Nokia NK402 Instructions

Screen prompts
The words you see at the bottom of the screen. Use the 'Navi Key' below to select these functions

'C' key
Press once to: 'Busy' an incoming call (divert to Answer Phone), delete text, or to return to the previous screen. Press and hold to delete all text displayed. And again hold to return to the main display

'1' key
Press and hold to automatically call your Answer Phone

Number keys
Used to enter numbers or text when typing in a name or number eg: press 2 once for 'A', twice for 'B', three times for 'C', and four times for '2'

'0' key
Press once to add a space between characters when entering numbers and text

'Star' key
Use this key to select special characters. Press twice to enter '+' when making international calls

Concealed Mouthpiece/Microphone

Phone Charger socket

Connector socket
Use this socket to connect to Handsfree Kits, Car Kits or data leads

Antenna

Earpiece

On/Off button (red)
Press and hold to switch on and off.
Press briefly when the display is clear or during a call, to choose 'Personal', 'Silent', 'Discreet' or 'Loud' tones (see Chapter 4). When pressed at other times, the lights are turned on for a few seconds

Backlit Display (main display)
Displays the word 'Orange' if service is available, the antenna signal strength and battery indicators. You can also set the time to be displayed

Navi Key
Use this all purpose key to make, answer and 'End' calls. When pressed at other times it performs the screen prompt function, or enters the menu, displayed on the screen

Scroll keys
Use these keys to scroll through menus, messages and your personal directory. During a call they act as volume keys. From the main display screen use to access a list of the last 8 dialled numbers and to go directly to your Phonebook

Hash/arrow key
Allows you to select either upper or lower case letters, and numbers, when entering text from the keypad. Press and hold to change from Line One to Line Two from the main display.

SCREEN SYMBOLS

Antenna
The more bars visible, the stronger the signal.

Battery level
The more bars visible, the more power in the battery.

 Phonebook

Text insertion symbol
Appears when entering names and numbers in a text message. When a number appears in the top right of the screen this is an indication of the number of remaining characters available.

Call in progress

ABC Upper case indicator

abc Lower case indicator

123 Numbers indicator

Active call

Call on hold

Answer Phone message received

Answer Phone message
Received on Line One.

Answer Phone message
Received on Line Two.

Text message received

Text message waiting to read

Text message already read

Line One Diverted

Line Two Diverted

Line One and Line Two Diverted

Silent mode (no ring selected)

Locked keypad
'Navi Key' then 'Star' Key to unlock

Line One indicator

Line Two indicator

Alarm clock set

MAKE A CALL

■ **make a call**
1 Press and hold the **On/Off** button on the front of your phone to switch it on.
2 The phone will beep once, search for a network and then display '**Orange**' when in the UK. When overseas a different network will be displayed.
3 Key in the number you want to call. Always use the full area code, even if the number is in your area.
4 Press the **Navi Key** when '**Call**' is displayed to call the number.

■ **end a call**
1 Press the **Navi Key** when '**End**' is displayed to hang up.

■ **how to redial the last number you called**
1 Press the up **Scroll Key** once.
The last number dialled and '**Call**' will be displayed. Use the **Scroll Key** to see the last ten numbers you dialled.

2 Select '**Call**' to call the number you have selected.

■ **keypad lock**
Because it's so easy to make a call using the Navi Key you can lock the keypad to avoid accidentally pressing keys when the phone is in a pocket or handbag.

■ Press the **Navi Key** followed by the ❁ key to lock the keypad. Repeat to unlock. Emergency calls can still be made and you can answer calls as normal but no other key presses will be accepted.
tip You can adjust the earpiece volume during a call by pressing ▲or ▼

ANSWER A CALL

■ **answer a call**

When your phone rings, simply press the **Navi Key** and start talking! Alternatively, with Orange, you have the choice to divert the call to your Answer Phone using the 'Busy' feature below. Press the **Navi Key** to hang up.

■ **Caller id**

When your phone rings, your caller's number will be displayed – if it is available from their network. If it is stored in the '**Phonebook**' menu, their name will be displayed instead.

If you don't answer an incoming call '**Missed call**' and '**List**' are displayed and the time, date and phone number details will be available by scrolling.

When you make a call your phone number will be sent, by the network, to the person you are calling. Key in **141** before each number you dial to withold this or write to Orange Customer Services to have your number continually withheld. (This also prevents you from receiving other peoples' Caller id).

■ **using the 'Busy' feature**

If you are unable or do not wish to answer a call you can divert it to your Answer Phone, using the 'Busy' feature.

■ **put a call on Hold**

During a call you may wish to speak privately to someone else, or make a second call. You can do this by using the '**Hold**' option from the 'In-Call Options' menu during a call.

1 During a call, press **C**.
2 Press '**Options**', '**End all calls**' is highlighted.
3 Scroll down to '**Hold**' and press '**Select**'. Repeat the process and scroll to '**Unhold**'.

■ **Call Waiting**

Call Waiting is a feature that sounds an audible alert when you are already on a call and someone else calls you. Select **Menu 4–1–3** and press '**OK**'. Scroll to '**On**' or '**Off**' and press '**OK**' again to select the one you want. When '**Call Waiting**' is set to '**On**' you can press '**OK**' to accept a second call.

CHARGE THE PHONE'S BATTERY

■ **attaching the battery**

1 Locate the battery runners in the grooves on the back of the phone.
2 Slide it upwards until it clicks into place.

■ **charging the battery**

The first couple of charges must be for at least 16 hours in order to achieve optimum performance. You can make calls whilst charging your phone.

Plug your charger into a mains socket. Insert the other end of the lead into the base of your phone. To confirm charging is in progress the battery indicator will start flashing within 20 seconds. Rechargeable batteries have a limited lifespan and Orange recommend that you purchase a new one every year.

■ **removing the battery**

Remove the battery by pressing the button at the top and sliding it down the phone.

■ **about the SIM Card**

Your SIM Card is a computer chip containing information about your phone and subscription. The card inserts under the battery. Used in another Orange phone it keeps your phone number and anything stored in its' memory. Your phone will not work without it and if you did not receive one when you bought your phone, contact your stockist or call Orange Customer Services.

■ **removing the SIM Card**

Slide up and swing open the SIM Card holder catch. Slide the SIM Card out of the holder.

Note: Always handle the SIM Card with care and insert with the golden contacts face down.

SEND A TEXT MESSAGE

- **send a text message**
  1. Press '**Menu**' then **2**. '**Inbox**' is displayed. Scroll to see the rest of the list: '**Outbox**', '**Write messages**' and '**Message settings**'.
  2. Scroll to '**Write messages**' and press '**Select**' to display the text input screen.
  3. Key in your message, up to 160 characters. (e.g. to get '**J**' press **5** once, to get '**S**' press **7** four times).
     - Use the **Scroll Key** to move the cursor along
     - Press C to delete characters if necessary
     - Press # to change from upper to lower case letters. Press and hold to change to numbers
     - Press * to display a list of special characters.
  4. When you have finished your message press '**Options**'. Scroll to the one you want and press '**OK**'.
     - **Send** – Allows you to enter the mobile number of the person you wish to send the message to.
     - **Save** – Allows you to save the message in your '**Outbox**' for later use
     - **Clear Screen**.
  5. To send a message to another mobile phone number scroll to '**Send**' and press '**OK**'.
  6. Enter the mobile number you wish to send the message to or press '**Search**' to go directly to your Phonebook.
  7. Scroll or enter the first letter of the name you want, then press '**OK**' twice. '**Message Sending**' is displayed.

- **confirm the receipt of a sent text message**
  When sending an important text message to another mobile phone, add 'RCT' to the beginning of the message. This requests a confirmation text message to be sent back to your phone when the text message is delivered. This is the only way of confirming receipt.

- **special characters**

key	lower case
1	Space – ? ! , . : ; * " ' < = > ( ) _ 1
2	A B C Å Ä Æ à Ç 2 °
3	D E F è É Δ Ê
4	G H I Ì 4
5	J K L 5 §
6	M N O Ñ Ö Ø ò 6
7	P Q R S ß 7 Π Σ
8	T U V Ü ù 8
9	W X Y Z 9
0	1 & @ / % $ £ ¥ ¿ i 0 • „ Ω

have fun with text messaging abbreviations

Too, to, two	2	Late	L8	What	WOT
For, four	4	Later	L8R	Kiss	X
Today	2DAY	Oh I see	OIC	Hugs & kisses	OXOXO
Tomorrow	2MORO	Please call me	PCM	Smiley face	:-)
All the best	ATB	Please	PLS	Confused face	%-)
Be	B	Are	R	Surprised face	:-o
Before	B4	You	U	Winking face	;-)
Be seeing you	BCNU	Thanks	THX	Sad face	:-(
See you	CU	Thank you	THNQ	Pig	:@)
Free to talk	F2T	What do you	WADYA	Anger	:-II
Great	GR8	Want to	WAN2	Tongue tied	:-&

MURDER MYSTERY

This task will allow students to achieve: **C3.1a, C3.1b, C3.2** as well as aspects of Working with Others.

AIM

To encourage teamwork and co-operation.

To develop discursive and argumentative skills.

To develop close-reading skills.

EQUIPMENT NEEDED

Each student needs a copy of one of the Murder Reports and a data sheet. Students may require pen and paper to make notes with.

GROUPING

Groups of five.

TIME

One lesson to solve the murder and one lesson to write up a Detectives' Report.

Task

This is a complex discussion task that requires real teamwork and co-operation. Students should work as a team to discover who committed the crime. The task can be extended to fulfil more key skills if you ask students to write up a Detectives' Report at the end of the task and include an image. Students should present their experience of working as a team to the rest of the class once the task is complete.

Teacher's Secret

Each of the murder reports contains slightly different information. Students must read through closely and share their reading to find this out. Keep the solution sheet close to your chest!

MURDER ONE SOLUTION SHEET

NAME	HEIGHT	WEIGHT (llbs)	AGE	BLOOD TYPE	OCCUPATION AT 7.30 PM (FREE TO MAKE PHONE CALL)	OCCUPATION AT 10 PM (FREE TO MAKE PHONE CALL)
Set Number	(4)	(2)	(2)	(3)	(5)	(1)
Viron, Benjamin ('Benjie')	5'4"*	220	49	B	Unknown	Unknown
Enopac, Alphonse ('Jumbo')	5' 7"	245	52	A*	Unknown	Unknown
Olleg, Joseph ('Chills')	5'71/2"	180*	52	A*	Near Social club	Unknown
Phelps, James ('Digger')	5'7"	210	52	B	Conducting Union Meeting*	Unknown
Sutter, Edward ('Blue Eyes')	5'7"	240	51	B	Near Social Club	Unknown
Lagas, Franklin ('Hot Dog')	5'7"	235	50	B	Near Offtrack Betting Office	In custody of joint task force*
Aifam, George ('Gypsy')	5'71/2"	245	39*	B	Near Offtrack Betting Office	Unknown

Note: The set number refers to the number of the information sheet where the clue is given. Items with an asterisk show why the suspect could not have committed the crime. All are eliminated except one.

◢ MURDER ONE INSTRUCTION SHEET

Instructions

1. You are a group of top detectives who have been assigned to the Organised Crime Bureau within your department.

2. The threat of violence between various factions of organised crime, over the control of narcotics, imperils the tranquillity of your community. To combat this threat, the commissioner has directed a step up in the activity against criminal organisations within your community.

3. Charly 'Poppa' Hasson's gang has been singled out for particular attention by your team.

4. Your task becomes complicated when a murder occurs during your investigation.

5. Your task, as a group, is to single out one suspect from members of the Hasson gang. Circumstantial evidence may be used to identify and arrest one member of the gang. The remaining six suspects must be cleared for a specific reason, which you as a group must declare at the termination of the activity. Data has been supplied regarding the suspects. Your team has all the information necessary for the solution of the case.

Assumptions

1. Assume that there is one solution.

2. Assume that all data is correct.

3. You have forty-five minutes in which to determine a suspect.

4. Assume that today's date is 7 July 1977 and that all primary actions are taking place on this date.

5. There must be substantial agreement in your group that the problem is solved.

6. You must work through the problem as a group.

Good Luck!

MURDER ONE BRIEFING SHEET 1

Charly 'Poppa' Hasson has been linked to organised crime by both Federal and State Organised Crime Task Forces. Information has been received that Charly Hasson has formed a gang of his own and is engaged in heavyweight narcotics traffic. Recent investigations by your department have disclosed the identity of seven members of the Hasson gang. Further investigations, and surveillance, have revealed that the members of the gang are actively engaged in narcotics distribution, despite severe pressure from the Joint Organised Task Force. Confidential information has disclosed a widening rift between gang members and Charly Hasson; members of the gang have accused him of 'skimming off the top'. Threats have been made by gang members to blow Charly away if he doesn't shape up.

As a result of the threats, Charly has been making himself scarce and rarely meets more than one gang member at a time. He has secluded himself in an apartment in a remote part of town, a relatively safe location unknown to the gang members. An informant has told your department about Hasson's hideout, and a legal wiretap has been installed on his telephone. Several days have gone by, and no action has been indicated by the tap. On 7 July, at 7.30pm, Charly made a call to an undetermined public phone booth, and a taped conversation was recorded as follows:

Unknown Person: *'Yeah?'*
Poppa (Charly):   *'Eh, I got a big one; meet me at the club at 10.30.'*
Unknown Person: *'OK.'* (Clicks off.)

Past information indicated the club to be the Starlight Hunting and Fishing Club at 197 Kenmore Street, a secluded place used in the past for gang meetings. Other persons have divulged that some heavyweight drugs have come into town. Thus, it appears that Charly may be getting a slice of the action. With this in mind, your squad C.O. decides to cover the club and put a close surveillance on all suspects at the location.

The Joint Task Force, having information confirming a big shipment to the city, swings into action at 9.00pm this date and simultaneously rounds up suspects who might be involved. The sweep nets twenty suspects including: Johnny Appleseed, Harry Hinge, Bruce Comma, Benny Carato, Frankie Lagas, Sam Perez, John Smith, Mike Crupa, Danny Skidmore, Frankie Todd, Sidney Hall, Jackie Leod and Cary Crooke. All are known by the department to be actively engaged in illegal narcotics traffic. The stakeout at Poppa's house reports that he leaves at 9.30pm but he loses the tail at about 10.00pm on the other side of town. Other tails report in and information about the members of Poppa's gang is compiled by the team. At 7.00pm surveillance had disclosed that Jumbo and Benjie's whereabouts were unknown, Hot Dog and Gypsy were near an offtrack betting office, Digger was at some meeting, and Chills and Blue Eyes were in the vicinity of a social club. Armed with this information, the team moves to 197 Kenmore Street.

At 10.15pm the first unit of the team arrives and observes that the club door is ajar and Hasson's car is parked outside. The area seems deserted, and only one light flickers through the open door. It appears from the outside that someone is lying on the floor. A decision is made to move in for a better look. Closer scrutiny reveals Charly's body lying face down on the floor. He is bleeding profusely from

head wounds, apparently gunshot wounds, from a weapon found lying near an open window at the rear of the premises. The area is immediately sealed off and the forensic unit is called to the scene. While awaiting the results of the lab unit, the team makes a door-to-door canvas in an attempt to locate a witness or persons who might have seen Charly with someone at the location.

The search is apparently fruitless until one middle-aged man is found who observed two men entering the abandoned club while he was walking his dog. The frightened witness, who resides three blocks from the club, says he saw two men enter the building and then heard a loud argument, during which someone shouted 'No! No!'. At that time he heard two shots and the door of the club opened but no one came out. Then he saw a man fleeing from behind the building. The man was middle-aged, wore a white shirt and black trousers, was about average in height and was heavy. The man fled in a dark sedan parked on the next block. The witness, fearful for his own life ran home, and when a detective doing door-to-door interviews came to his house, the witness gave him the above information.

The forensic unit thoroughly searches the premises and comes up with prints belonging to Charly; other prints are not distinguishable and cannot be classified. The weapon located at the scene is a .44 magnum of undetermined origin; no prints are obtained from the gun. Blood stains seem to indicate a fierce struggle, and apparently Charly had almost made it to the door. The blood stains on the floor fall into two groupings: A and B. Charly had bled profusely and beneath his fingernails are tufts of hair. Further investigation revealed a footprint in the tomato patch below the window at the rear of the club. The print seems to be anywhere from a size 7 to a size 8; it is somewhat distorted and was made by a man of greater than average weight. (This is determined by a mould made at the scene and a measurement of the height of the drop from the window to the ground.) Pressure from the hierarchy of the department demands a quick solution to this case, especially in view of the recent mass arrests made by the Joint Task Force. On the basis of the facts herein your team is directed to make a prompt arrest.

The most likely suspects are the members of Charly 'Poppa' Hasson's gang. It would seem likely that Charly called a member of the gang and made an appointment with his killer. All the information available to your team can be pulled from the Briefing Sheet. Your task is to identify the killer by using the facts available.

MURDER ONE BRIEFING SHEET 2

Charly 'Poppa' Hasson has been linked to organised crime by both Federal and State Organised Crime Task Forces. Information has been received that Poppa Hasson has formed a gang of his own and is engaged in heavyweight narcotics traffic. Recent investigations by your department have disclosed the identity of seven members of the Hasson gang. Further investigations, and surveillance, have revealed that the members of the gang are actively engaged in narcotics distribution, despite severe pressure from the Joint Organised Task Force. Confidential information has disclosed a widening rift between gang members and Charly Hasson; members of the gang have accused him of 'skimming off the top'. Threats have been made by gang members to blow Charly away if he doesn't shape up.

As a result of the threats, Charly has been making himself scarce and rarely meets more than one gang member at a time. He has secluded himself in an apartment in a remote part of town, a relatively safe location unknown to the gang members. An informant has told your department about Hasson's hideout, and a legal wiretap has been installed on his telephone. Several days have gone by, and no action has been indicated by the tap. On 7 July, at 7.30pm, Charly made a call to an undetermined public phone booth, and a taped conversation was recorded as follows:

Unknown Person: *'Yeah?'*
Poppa (Charly):   *'Eh, I got a big one; meet me at the club at 10.30.'*
Unknown Person: *'OK.'* (Clicks off.)

Past information indicated the club to be the Starlight Hunting and Fishing Club at 197 Kenmore Street, a secluded place used in the past for gang meetings. Other persons have divulged that some heavyweight drugs have come into town. Thus, it appears that Charly may be getting a slice of the action. With this in mind, your squad C.O. decides to cover the club and put a close surveillance on all suspects at the location.

The Joint Task Force, having information confirming a big shipment to the city, swings into action at 9.00pm this date and simultaneously rounds up suspects who might be involved. The sweep nets twenty suspects including: Johnny Appleseed, Harry Hinge, Bruce Comma, Benny Carato, Sam Perez, John Smith, Mike Crupa, Danny Skidmore, Frankie Todd, Sidney Hall, Jackie Leod and Cary Crooke. All are known by the department to be actively engaged in illegal narcotics traffic. The stakeout at Poppa's house reports that he leaves at 9.30pm but he loses the tail at about 10.00pm on the other side of town. Other tails report in and information about the members of Poppa's gang is compiled by the team. At 7.00pm surveillance had disclosed that Jumbo and Benjie's whereabouts were unknown, Hot Dog and Gypsy were near an offtrack betting office, Digger was at some meeting, and Chills and Blue Eyes were in the vicinity of a social club. Armed with this information, the team moves to 197 Kenmore Street.

At 10.15pm the first unit of the team arrives and observes that the club door is ajar and Hasson's car is parked outside. The area seems deserted, and only one light flickers through the open door. It appears from the outside that someone is lying on the floor. A decision is made to move in for a better look. Closer scrutiny reveals Charly's body lying face down on the floor. He is bleeding profusely from

head wounds, apparently gunshot wounds, from a weapon found lying near an open window at the rear of the premises. The area is immediately sealed off and the forensic unit is called to the scene. While awaiting the results of the lab unit, the team makes a door-to-door canvas in an attempt to locate a witness or persons who might have seen Charly with someone at the location.

The search is apparently fruitless until one middle-aged man is found who observed two men entering the abandoned club while he was walking his dog. The frightened witness, who resides three blocks from the club, says he saw two men enter the building and then heard a loud argument, during which someone shouted 'No! No!'. At that time he heard two shots and the door of the club opened but no one came out. Then he saw a man fleeing from behind the building. The man was about fifty, wore a white shirt and black trousers, was about average in height and was heavy. The man fled in a dark sedan parked on the next block. The witness, fearful for his own life ran home, and when a detective doing door-to-door interviews came to his house, the witness gave him the above information.

The forensic unit thoroughly searches the premises and comes up with prints belonging to Charly; other prints are not distinguishable and cannot be classified. The weapon located at the scene is a .44 magnum of undetermined origin; no prints are obtained from the gun. Blood stains seem to indicate a fierce struggle, and apparently Charly had almost made it to the door. The blood stains on the floor fall into two groupings: A and B. Charly had bled profusely and beneath his fingernails are tufts of hair. Further investigation revealed a footprint in the tomato patch below the window at the rear of the club. The print seems to be anywhere from a size 7 to a size 8; it is somewhat distorted and was made by a man of over two hundred pounds in weight. (This is determined by a mould made at the scene and a measurement of the height of the drop from the window to the ground.) Pressure from the hierarchy of the department demands a quick solution to this case, especially in view of the recent mass arrests made by the Joint Task Force. On the basis of the facts herein your team is directed to make a prompt arrest.

The most likely suspects are the members of Charly 'Poppa' Hasson's gang. It would seem likely that Charly called a member of the gang and made an appointment with his killer. All the information available to your team can be pulled from the Briefing Sheet. Your task is to identify the killer by using the facts available.

MURDER ONE BRIEFING SHEET 3

Charly 'Poppa' Hasson has been linked to organised crime by both Federal and State Organised Crime Task Forces. Information has been received that Poppa Hasson has formed a gang of his own and is engaged in heavyweight narcotics traffic. Recent investigations by your department have disclosed the identity of seven members of the Hasson gang. Further investigations, and surveillance, have revealed that the members of the gang are actively engaged in narcotics distribution, despite severe pressure from the Joint Organised Task Force. Confidential information has disclosed a widening rift between gang members and Charly Hasson; members of the gang have accused him of 'skimming off the top'. Threats have been made by gang members to blow Charly away if he doesn't shape up.

As a result of the threats, Charly has been making himself scarce and rarely meets more than one gang member at a time. He has secluded himself in an apartment in a remote part of town, a relatively safe location unknown to the gang members. An informant has told your department about Hasson's hideout, and a legal wiretap has been installed on his telephone. Several days have gone by, and no action has been indicated by the tap. On 7 July, at 7.30pm, Charly made a call to an undetermined public phone booth, and a taped conversation was recorded as follows:

Unknown Person: *'Yeah?'*
Poppa (Charly):   *'Eh, I got a big one; meet me at the club at 10.30.'*
Unknown Person: *'OK.'* (Clicks off.)

Past information indicated the club to be the Starlight Hunting and Fishing Club at 197 Kenmore Street, a secluded place used in the past for gang meetings. Other persons have divulged that some heavyweight drugs have come into town. Thus, it appears that Charly may be getting a slice of the action. With this in mind, your squad C.O. decides to cover the club and put a close surveillance on all suspects at the location.

The Joint Task Force, having information confirming a big shipment to the city, swings into action at 9.00pm this date and simultaneously rounds up suspects who might be involved. The sweep nets twenty suspects including: Johnny Appleseed, Harry Hinge, Bruce Comma, Benny Carato, Sam Perez, John Smith, Mike Crupa, Danny Skidmore, Frankie Todd, Sidney Hall, Jackie Leod and Cary Crooke. All are known by the department to be actively engaged in illegal narcotics traffic. The stakeout at Poppa's house reports that he leaves at 9.30pm but he loses the tail at about 10.00pm on the other side of town. Other tails report in and information about the members of Poppa's gang is compiled by the team. At 7.00pm surveillance had disclosed that Jumbo and Benjie's whereabouts were unknown, Hot Dog and Gypsy were near an offtrack betting office, Digger was at some meeting, and Chills and Blue Eyes were in the vicinity of a social club. Armed with this information, the team moves to 197 Kenmore Street.

At 10.15pm the first unit of the team arrives and observes that the club door is ajar and Hasson's car is parked outside. The area seems deserted, and only one light flickers through the open door. It appears from the outside that someone is lying on the floor. A decision is made to move in for a better look. Closer scrutiny reveals Charly's body lying face down on the floor. He is bleeding profusely from

head wounds, apparently gunshot wounds, from a weapon found lying near an open window at the rear of the premises. The area is immediately sealed off and the forensic unit is called to the scene. While awaiting the results of the lab unit, the team makes a door-to-door canvas in an attempt to locate a witness or persons who might have seen Charly with someone at the location.

The search is apparently fruitless until one middle-aged man is found who observed two men entering the abandoned club while he was walking his dog. The frightened witness, who resides three blocks from the club, says he saw two men enter the building and then heard a loud argument, during which someone shouted 'No! No!'. At that time he heard two shots and the door of the club opened but no one came out. Then he saw a man fleeing from behind the building. The man was middle-aged, wore a white shirt and black trousers, was about average in height and was heavy. The man fled in a dark sedan parked on the next block. The witness, fearful for his own life ran home, and when a detective doing door-to-door interviews came to his house, the witness gave him the above information.

The forensic unit thoroughly searches the premises and comes up with prints belonging to Charly; other prints are not distinguishable and cannot be classified. The weapon located at the scene is a .44 magnum of undetermined origin; no prints are obtained from the gun. Blood stains seem to indicate a fierce struggle, and apparently Charly had almost made it to the door. The blood stains on the floor fall into two groupings: A and B. Charly had bled profusely; he had blood type A. Beneath his fingernails are tufts of hair. Further investigation revealed a footprint in the tomato patch below the window at the rear of the club. The print seems to be anywhere from a size 7 to a size 8; it is somewhat distorted and was made by a man of greater than average weight. (This is determined by a mould made at the scene and a measurement of the height of the drop from the window to the ground.) Pressure from the hierarchy of the department demands a quick solution to this case, especially in view of the recent mass arrests made by the Joint Task Force. On the basis of the facts herein your team is directed to make a prompt arrest.

The most likely suspects are the members of Charly 'Poppa' Hasson's gang. It would seem likely that Charly called a member of the gang and made an appointment with his killer. All the information available to your team can be pulled from the Briefing Sheet. Your task is to identify the killer by using the facts available.

MURDER ONE BRIEFING SHEET 4

Charly 'Poppa' Hasson has been linked to organised crime by both Federal and State Organised Crime Task Forces. Information has been received that Poppa Hasson has formed a gang of his own and is engaged in heavyweight narcotics traffic. Recent investigations by your department have disclosed the identity of seven members of the Hasson gang. Further investigations, and surveillance, have revealed that the members of the gang are actively engaged in narcotics distribution, despite severe pressure from the Joint Organised Task Force. Confidential information has disclosed a widening rift between gang members and Charly Hasson; members of the gang have accused him of 'skimming off the top'. Threats have been made by gang members to blow Charly away if he doesn't shape up.

As a result of the threats, Charly has been making himself scarce and rarely meets more than one gang member at a time. He has secluded himself in an apartment in a remote part of town, a relatively safe location unknown to the gang members. An informant has told your department about Hasson's hideout, and a legal wiretap has been installed on his telephone. Several days have gone by, and no action has been indicated by the tap. On 7 July, at 7.30pm, Charly made a call to an undetermined public phone booth, and a taped conversation was recorded as follows:

Unknown Person: 'Yeah?'
Poppa (Charly): 'Eh, I got a big one; meet me at the club at 10.30.'
Unknown Person: 'OK.' (Clicks off.)

Past information indicated the club to be the Starlight Hunting and Fishing Club at 197 Kenmore Street, a secluded place used in the past for gang meetings. Other persons have divulged that some heavyweight drugs have come into town. Thus, it appears that Charly may be getting a slice of the action. With this in mind, your squad C.O. decides to cover the club and put a close surveillance on all suspects at the location.

The Joint Task Force, having information confirming a big shipment to the city, swings into action at 9.00pm this date and simultaneously rounds up suspects who might be involved. The sweep nets twenty suspects including: Johnny Appleseed, Harry Hinge, Bruce Comma, Benny Carato, Sam Perez, John Smith, Mike Crupa, Danny Skidmore, Frankie Todd, Sidney Hall, Jackie Leod and Cary Crooke. All are known by the department to be actively engaged in illegal narcotics traffic. The stakeout at Poppa's house reports that he leaves at 9.30pm but he loses the tail at about 10.00pm on the other side of town. Other tails report in and information about the members of Poppa's gang is compiled by the team. At 7.00pm surveillance had disclosed that Jumbo and Benjie's whereabouts were unknown, Hot Dog and Gypsy were near an offtrack betting office, Digger was at some meeting, and Chills and Blue Eyes were in the vicinity of a social club. Armed with this information, the team moves to 197 Kenmore Street.

At 10.15pm the first unit of the team arrives and observes that the club door is ajar and Hasson's car is parked outside. The area seems deserted, and only one light flickers through the open door. It appears from the outside that someone is lying on the floor. A decision is made to move in for a better look. Closer scrutiny reveals Charly's body lying face down on the floor. He is bleeding profusely from

head wounds, apparently gunshot wounds, from a weapon found lying near an open window at the rear of the premises. The area is immediately sealed off and the forensic unit is called to the scene. While awaiting the results of the lab unit, the team makes a door-to-door canvas in an attempt to locate a witness or persons who might have seen Charly with someone at the location.

The search is apparently fruitless until one middle-aged man is found who observed two men entering the abandoned club while he was walking his dog. The frightened witness, who resides three blocks from the club, says he saw two men enter the building and then heard a loud argument, during which someone shouted 'No! No!'. At that time he heard two shots and the door of the club opened but no one came out. Then he saw a man fleeing from behind the building. The man was middle-aged, wore a white shirt and black trousers, was about five feet seven, and was heavy. The man fled in a dark sedan parked on the next block. The witness, fearful for his own life ran home, and when a detective doing door-to-door interviews came to his house, the witness gave him the above information.

The forensic unit thoroughly searches the premises and comes up with prints belonging to Charly; other prints are not distinguishable and cannot be classified. The weapon located at the scene is a .44 magnum of undetermined origin; no prints are obtained from the gun. Blood stains seem to indicate a fierce struggle, and apparently Charly had almost made it to the door. The blood stains on the floor fall into two groupings: A and B. Charly had bled profusely and beneath his fingernails are tufts of hair. Further investigation revealed a footprint in the tomato patch below the window at the rear of the club. The print seems to be anywhere from a size 7 to a size 8; it is somewhat distorted and was made by a man of greater than average weight. (This is determined by a mould made at the scene and a measurement of the height of the drop from the window to the ground.) Pressure from the hierarchy of the department demands a quick solution to this case, especially in view of the recent mass arrests made by the Joint Task Force. On the basis of the facts herein your team is directed to make a prompt arrest.

The most likely suspects are the members of Charly 'Poppa' Hasson's gang. It would seem likely that Charly called a member of the gang and made an appointment with his killer. All the information available to your team can be culled from the Briefing Sheet. Your task is to identify the killer by using the facts available.

MURDER ONE BRIEFING SHEET 5

Charly 'Poppa' Hasson has been linked to organised crime by both Federal and State Organised Crime Task Forces. Information has been received that Poppa Hasson has formed a gang of his own and is engaged in heavyweight narcotics traffic. Recent investigations by your department have disclosed the identity of seven members of the Hasson gang. Further investigations, and surveillance, have revealed that the members of the gang are actively engaged in narcotics distribution, despite severe pressure from the Joint Organised Task Force. Confidential information has disclosed a widening rift between gang members and Charly Hasson; members of the gang have accused him of 'skimming off the top'. Threats have been made by gang members to blow Charly away if he doesn't shape up.

As a result of the threats, Charly has been making himself scarce and rarely meets more than one gang member at a time. He has secluded himself in an apartment in a remote part of town, a relatively safe location unknown to the gang members. An informant has told your department about Hasson's hideout, and a legal wiretap has been installed on his telephone. Several days have gone by, and no action has been indicated by the tap. On 7 July, at 7.30pm, Charly made a call to an undetermined public phone booth, and a taped conversation was recorded as follows:

Unknown Person: 'Yeah?'
Poppa (Charly):   'Eh, I got a big one; meet me at the club at 10.30.'
Unknown Person: 'OK.' (Clicks off.)

Past information indicated the club to be the Starlight Hunting and Fishing Club at 197 Kenmore Street, a secluded place used in the past for gang meetings. Other persons have divulged that some heavyweight drugs have come into town. Thus, it appears that Charly may be getting a slice of the action. With this in mind, your squad C.O. decides to cover the club and put a close surveillance on all suspects at the location.

The Joint Task Force, having information confirming a big shipment to the city, swings into action at 9.00pm this date and simultaneously rounds up suspects who might be involved. The sweep nets twenty suspects including: Johnny Appleseed, Harry Hinge, Bruce Comma, Benny Carato, Sam Perez, John Smith, Mike Crupa, Danny Skidmore, Frankie Todd, Sidney Hall, Jackie Leod and Cary Crooke. All are known by the department to be actively engaged in illegal narcotics traffic. The stakeout at Poppa's house reports that he leaves at 9.30pm but he loses the tail at about 10.00pm on the other side of town. Other tails report in and information about the members of Poppa's gang is compiled by the team. At 7.00pm surveillance had disclosed that Jumbo and Benjie's whereabouts were unknown, Hot Dog and Gypsy were near an offtrack betting office, Digger was conducting a union meeting, and Chills and Blue Eyes were in the vicinity of a social club. Armed with this information, the team move to 197 Kenmore Street.

At 10.15pm the first unit of the team arrives and observes that the club door is ajar and Hasson's car is parked outside. The area seems deserted, and only one light flickers through the open door. It appears from the outside that someone is lying on the floor. A decision is made to move in for a better look. Closer scrutiny reveals Charly's body lying face down on the floor. He is bleeding profusely from

head wounds, apparently gunshot wounds, from a weapon found lying near an open window at the rear of the premises. The area is immediately sealed off and the forensic unit is called to the scene. While awaiting the results of the lab unit, the team makes a door-to-door canvas in an attempt to locate a witness or persons who might have seen Charly with someone at the location.

The search is apparently fruitless until one middle-aged man is found who observed two men entering the abandoned club while he was walking his dog. The frightened witness, who resides three blocks from the club, says he saw two men enter the building and then heard a loud argument, during which someone shouted 'No! No!'. At that time he heard two shots and the door of the club opened but no one came out. Then he saw a man fleeing from behind the building. The man was middle-aged, wore a white shirt and black trousers, was about average in height and was heavy. The man fled in a dark sedan parked on the next block. The witness, fearful for his own life ran home, and when a detective doing door-to-door interviews came to his house, the witness gave him the above information.

The forensic unit thoroughly searches the premises and comes up with prints belonging to Charly; other prints are not distinguishable and cannot be classified. The weapon located at the scene is a .44 magnum of undetermined origin; no prints obtained from the gun. Blood stains seem to indicate a fierce struggle, and apparently Charly had almost made it to the door. The blood stains on the floor fall into two groupings: A and B. Charly had bled profusely and beneath his fingernails are tufts of hair. Further investigation revealed a footprint in the tomato patch below the window at the rear of the club. The print seems to be anywhere from a size 7 to a size 8; it is somewhat distorted and was made by a man of greater than average weight. (This is determined by a mould made at the scene and a measurement of the height of the drop from the window to the ground.) Pressure from the hierarchy of the department demands a quick solution to this case, especially in view of the recent mass arrests made by the Joint Task Force. On the basis of the facts herein your team is directed to make a prompt arrest.

The most likely suspects are the members of Charly 'Poppa' Hasson's gang. It would seem likely that Charly called a member of the gang and made an appointment with his killer. All the information available to your team can be culled from the Briefing Sheet. Your task is to identify the killer by using the facts available.

MURDER ONE SUSPECT DATA SHEET

Viron, Benjamin ('Benjie')
Height: 5'4" Weight: 220 llbs Age: 49
Blood Type: B Shoe: 7½ Hair: Grey/Brown
Vehicle: 1973 Mercedes Dark Blue Sedan Eyes: Brown
Record: 17 arrests Tattoos: Right Arm, 'Mother'
Charges: Gambling, Assault, Narcotics, Loansharking, Extortion, Robbery, Rape.

Enopac, Alphonse ('Jumbo')
Height: 5'7" Weight: 245 llbs Age: 52
Blood Type: A Shoe: 8 Hair: Black/Grey
Vehicle: 1974 Lincoln Black Sedan Eyes: Brown
Record: 26 arrests Tattoos: Left Arm, 'Al & Eloise'
Charges: Gambling, Assault, Statutory Rapc, Narcotics, Extortion, Homicide.

Ollag, Joseph ('Chills')
Height: 5'7½" Weight: 180 llbs Age: 52
Blood Type: A Shoe: 8 Hair: Brown
Vehicle: 1972 Cadillac Black Sedan Eyes: Brown
Record: 20 arrests Tattoos: None
Charges: Gambling, Narcotics, Assault, Extortion, Homicide.

Phelps, James ('Digger')
Height: 5'7" Weight: 210 llbs Age: 52
Blood Type: B Shoe: 7½ Hair: Black/Brown
Vehicle: 1973 Cadillac Dark Green Sedan Eyes: Blue
Record: 30 arrests Tattoos: Chest, 'Blue Birds'
Charges: Gambling, Narcotics, Assault, Robbery, Loansharking, Homicide.

Sutter, Edward ('Blue Eyes')
Height: 5'7" Weight: 240 llbs Age: 51
Blood Type: B Shoe: 7½ Hair: Black/Grey
Vehicle: 1974 Chrysler Black Sedan Eyes: Brown
Record: 12 arrests Tattoos: Right Arm, 'For God and
Charges: Gambling, Loansharking, Country'
Assault, Rape, Extortion.

Lagas, Franklin ('Hot Dog')
Height: 5'7" Weight: 235 llbs Age: 50
Blood Type: B Shoe: 8 Hair: Black/Grey
Vehicle: 1973 Cadillac Black Sedan Eyes: Brown
Record: 19 arrests Tattoos: None
Charges: Homicide, Robbery, Assault, Extortion, Narcotics, Gambling, Impairing
Morals of a Minor.

Aifam, George ('Gypsy')
Height: 5'7½" Weight: 245 llbs Age: 39
Blood Type: B Shoe: 8 Hair: Black
Vehicle: 1973 Lincoln Black Sedan Eyes: Brown
Record: 23 arrests Tattoos: Left Arm, 'To Mother with
Charges: Gambling, Loansharking, Love'
Assault, Extortion, Homicide.

IMPROVE THE COLLEGE FACILITIES

This task enables students to earn Key Skill C3.1a and C3.1b.
If students submit their argument in writing they will also have one piece of evidence for their portfolio of writing, C3.3.

AIM

To develop debating skills.

EQUIPMENT NEEDED

One copy of each of the suggestion sheets and the task sheet per group.

GROUPING

Individual presentations or group presentations, (whichever seems the most appropriate to the student's needs and skills at this point in the course). There are sufficient suggestions for six groups.

TIME

One session to prepare the debate.

One session to hold the meeting.

IMPROVE THE COLLEGE FACILITIES

TASK

Your College has been awarded £200 000 by the Lottery. This is a large sum of money and it has been decided to spend it in a way which will benefit the maximum number of Sixth Form students. The College management have asked for suggestions to be submitted to them in writing and have shortlisted six ideas from all the suggestions which they received.

There is to be a meeting at the end of this week where a vote will be taken to decide how the money is to be spent. The money cannot be divided between two options. Staff and students have been invited to attend the meeting and the proposers of the six suggestions have been asked to speak for five minutes about their idea. They must explain how they intend to spend the money and how it will benefit the maximum number of students. There will be time for the proposals to be debated before the meeting votes to decide which suggestion the college will adopt. No new ideas will be accepted at this stage.

Your suggestion for spending the money has been shortlisted and you have been asked to speak at the meeting to explain your idea more fully. On the following pages are some notes which will help you, but you are allowed to add extra ideas of your own. You must be as persuasive as possible and you must be prepared to answer questions from the audience.

Your job is to choose one of the six suggestions on the following pages and present it to the meeting as if it is your own idea. You will need to expand on the information in order to develop your argument. You can provide whatever additional information you require to add weight to your argument.

You can work on this task as an individual presenter or you can put forward a group presentation. Whichever you choose, you must use an image to fulfil the requirement of Key Skill C3.1b.

This means that you will have to use a picture, a diagram or architect's drawing as part of your talk. You might want to present some facts and figures in the form of a table. Your choice of image is up to you.

You can use the information on debating presented in previous worksheets, and organise the meeting as a public debate. In this case you will need to elect a chairperson and a timekeeper.

When everyone has had time to prepare their presentation, the speakers take turns in putting forward their idea to the audience. At the end of the session, the audience will vote on which suggestion to adopt.

SUGGESTION 1
ADDITIONAL LIBRARY FACILITIES

The library at your College is a very popular place for students to work in. It has 35 computers and additional seating for 100 people. The College has 850 students at present and that number is expected to rise over the next five years.

Students find that if they do not get to the library as early as possible, all the places are taken and there is nowhere for them to work. Adjoining the library are four classrooms which are presently used by the English department. It is proposed to resite the English department elsewhere in the college and use the rooms to extend the working area of the library.

The work would be carried out over the summer holidays causing minimum disruption to the college and the students. Four walls would need to be demolished so that the classrooms would then form part of the library. This would effectively double the size of the library.

In addition to its use as a library, the area could then be used for staff meetings and for parents' evenings.

⚡ SUGGESTION 2
A DESIGNATED AREA FOR SMOKERS

Your College is a smoke-free workplace. This decision was taken by students over five years ago. The decision applies equally to students and staff. No smoking is permitted in classrooms, in corridors or in the staffrooms.

It is accepted that there are some students and staff who do smoke and this is tolerated in one small area, known as Smokers' Corner, situated at the north eastern edge of the building where there is a covered walkway leading to the perimeter of the college. This is a cold and draughty place, and is understandably unpopular with some students.

Over the past couple of years, smokers have begun to congregate at the bottom of one of the staircases adjacent to Smokers' Corner. This is increasingly becoming a nuisance to the college as the area attracts petty acts of vandalism such as damage to the fire extinguishers and damage to the nearby toilets.

The £200 000 could be used to provide a place where staff and students could go to smoke in comfort.

SUGGESTION 3
IMPROVED CANTEEN FACILITIES

The college canteen is used as a meeting place by the students as well as a place to eat and drink. Like most educational establishments the catering is franchised out to a company, called 'Caterlot', who have their own staff. The profits from all the food and drink sold on the college premises goes straight to Caterlot, who pay rent to the college.

The canteen is very popular with the students as they have no other common room. It is a place where they can meet between lessons and catch up with all the college gossip.

The canteen area where food is consumed, is too small for all the students who want to use it, but the kitchens are roomy enough to double their present capacity for producing food. It is proposed to enlarge the seating area of the canteen by building over a small area of the staff car park. This would give the students more room to meet and eat.

SUGGESTION 4
A NEW STUDENT COMMON ROOM

The College has a thriving Student Union with elected officers and a committee. There are student events at least once a month which are very well supported. Until two years ago there was a student common room next to the student union office but this had to close to make way for a Learning Centre. Some staff felt that the common room was under used and there had been some petty theft from the student union office. It is proposed to build a brand new area where students can meet to chat.

This would have the additional benefit of reducing the pressure on the canteen facilities which are already overstretched. Students who only wanted to chat could go to the common room, leaving the canteen for students who wanted a snack or a meal.

SUGGESTION 5
ADDITIONAL COMPUTING FACILITIES

The college is aware that it has only 250 computers for its 850 students. The computing facilities at the college are very well used. All students have to take a CLAIT course and Key Skills ICT.

All the college computers have an Internet facility and all students have an e-mail address. All the departments have been encouraged to build in as much ICT into their course as possible but it is not always easy for students to have access to the college computers. The computers are often in demand for lessons.

In addition, the college had begun to offer computer awareness sessions to a local employer. This means that more of the machines are being used during the college day, and all too frequently students have to wait for several hours for a computer to become free for them to use.

It is proposed to spend the money on additional computers which will not be used for teaching. They will be sited in the library and will be solely for Sixth Form students to use in their study periods.

⁄⁄ SUGGESTION 6
COVERED WALKWAYS BETWEEN BUILDINGS

The College was built more than fifty years ago. Originally there were five teaching areas in three blocks which surround a central car park. Over the years, the college has expanded into 'temporary' buildings, which are portable classrooms known as the 'huts'. These have been sited wherever there is sufficient space for them, but the majority are clustered around the car park.

The canteen and the library are both in separate buildings reached by walking across the car park.

On a sunny day, the journey from lesson to lesson is quite pleasant, but in the rain it can be a nightmare.

It is proposed to build a covered walkway around the perimetcr of the car park so that sludents and staff can reach all areas of the college without getting soaked on rainy days.

LONDON MARATHON

This task allows students to achieve Key Skills C3.1a, C3.1b and prepares students for C3.2.

AIM

To plan a group activity.

EQUIPMENT NEEDED

One copy of each pupil sheet per group.

A copy of a map of the London underground (not provided)

GROUPING

Groups of between three and five.

TIME

One hour to become familiar with the materials.

One hour to plan the day.

One hour to present the group's plan to the class.

LONDON MARATHON

TASK

One of your friends is taking part in the London Marathon for the first time. You are going to travel to London to support them. You want to be there at the start and at the finish, but you would like to see your friend as many times as possible on the route just to cheer them on. Your task is to plan your day and then present your schedule to the class. You will need to explain where you plan to meet your friend and why you have chosen your meeting points.

You know that your friend is running with the Whizz-Kidz and will be wearing the Whizz-Kidz running outfit. You know that there will be at least 30 000 runners on the day, so you will have to make careful arrangements if you are to meet up with your friend, otherwise you might miss her in all the crowds of runners.

Your friend is planning to finish the marathon by 2.00pm. She has been issued with the number 46,559.

You will need to plan your route carefully as you will be using public transport to go from one point to another. Try to take advantage of the Whizz-Kidz cheering squads because they will be easy for your friend to spot. Remember to leave enough time to get from place to place. You can use the time chart to see how quickly your friend will cover the course. Use a map of the London Underground to help you work out your route. You will need to explain which underground stations you plan to use when you report your ideas to the class at the end of this exercise.

When you are happy that you have arranged to see your friend as many times as possible, use one of the Marathon route maps or produce one of your own to illustrate your schedule. You can then use this as your image when you present your schedule to the class.

THE PERFECTLY KIT'D OUT RUNNER!

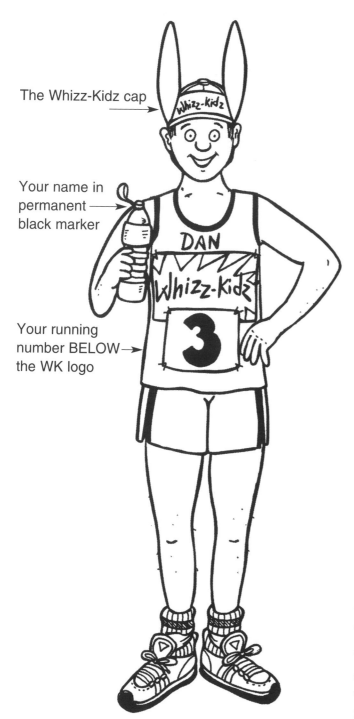

The Whizz-Kidz cap

Your name in permanent black marker

Your running number BELOW the WK logo

DAN

Whizz-Kidz

3

You'll be astonished and delighted with the crowd support yelled *specially for you* when you write your name above the WK logo – so get your permanent black marker out!

With your Whizz-Kidz running vest, your Whizz-Kidz running cap and your PUMA Blyss running shoes *(if you've sent in your sponsorship target already)* you are going to be one of the best dressed marathon runners out there!

We want to make sure that you make the most of our fabulous kit so please use this excellent drawing to ensure that you really look the business! Making sure that your Whizz-Kidz logo is showing clearly, and wearing your cap, will help to make the most of this fantastic PR opportunity and allow our extremely loud cheerers to spot you!

Remember

Try to **run on the left** at all times. The Whizz-Kidz cheering squads will be located on the **left hand side** of the road and due to the massive volume of runner and supporters on the day we might easily miss you if you are running on the right.

The WK Cheering Squads will be scanning the route for the bright WK vest logo and the WK hat. If you're not wearing either, you might easily be missed!

Text from pp58–63 is from the 'London Marathon booklet', Whizz-Kidz

THE TEAM PHOTO

Where?

The Whizz-Kidz Flora London Marathon 2000 Team photo will be held at the **Greenwich Park Bandstand**. The bandstand is right next to the RED START in Greenwich Park and it would be great to see you there. Just look out for the bright yellow banners and balloons.

When?

We will meet you at 8:00am for an 8:15am photo. Please turn up in full Whizz-Kidz kit with your *biggest* smiles for the camera! (If you would like a copy of the Team Photo, once developed, we would ask you to make a small donation to cover the cost.)

Location Map

Greenwich Park Bandstand

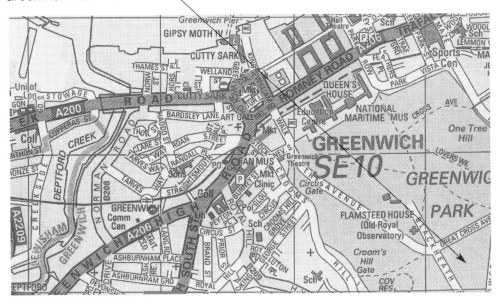

⫽ RECOVERY RECEPTION

Texas Embassy Cantina
1 Cockspur Street
Trafalgar Square
London
SW1Y 5DL

We'll have a team of masseurs reach to soothe your aches and pains after your tremendous achievement. They will operate a waiting list service so as soon as you arrive go and put your name down and make sure you stay nearby to listen out for your name or number to be called. Just think of the relaxing bliss of a ½ hour massage as you round the corner onto the Mall! There will be a massive plate of free food and a drink for that much needed carbo re-loading as well as plenty of congratulations.

The Texas Embassy Cantina is a great place for you to meet up with your friends and family. The race finish will be incredibly overcrowded – over 30,000 runners trying to meet up with friends and family members – so we definitely recommend you meet them at the Texas Embassy Cantina.

Map & Directions

Nearest tube and rail is Charing Cross.

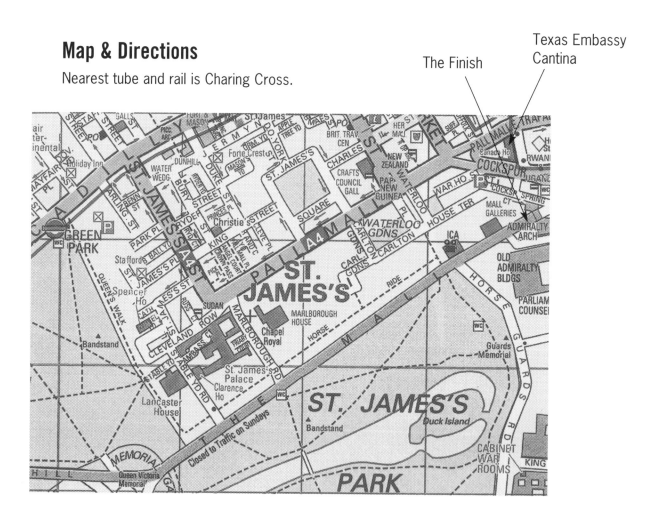

BRING YOUR FRIEND AND FAMILY ALONG TO CHEER

If your nearest and dearest want to be assured of catching that fleeting glimpse of you as you *zoom* past, then why not ask them to join a Whizz-Kidz cheering squad? The points we will be at are:

Mile 5   – Woolwich Road, walk from the start
Mile 11 – Brunell Road roundabout, tube: Rotherhithe
Mile 13 – Tower Bridge, tube/rail: London Bridge, Whizz-Kidz cheering point
Mile 14 – The Highway, rail: Limehouse DLR
Mile 18 – East Ferry Road, rail: Crossharbour DLR
Mile 22 – Tower Thistle, tube: Tower Hill
Mile 24 – Embankment, tube: Temple, rail: Blackfriars
Mile 26 – The Strand, tube: Charing Cross

We will have 8 different cheering points along the route but the best group for people to join is the one that goes from the start. If your supporters join this group, with Meurig and Xanne at Greenwich Park Bandstand, we will take them to **MILE 5** and **MILE 18**, so they should see you twice!

The benefits of joining the Whizz-Kidz cheering squad:

- Your friends and family will see you twice.
- We make so much noise you won't miss them.
- Our banners and balloons make us easy to spot.
- Your supporters won't get lost in the crowd!
- Whizz-Kidz have chosen cheering points where you really need them.

Map for Greenwich Park Bandstand & Mile 5

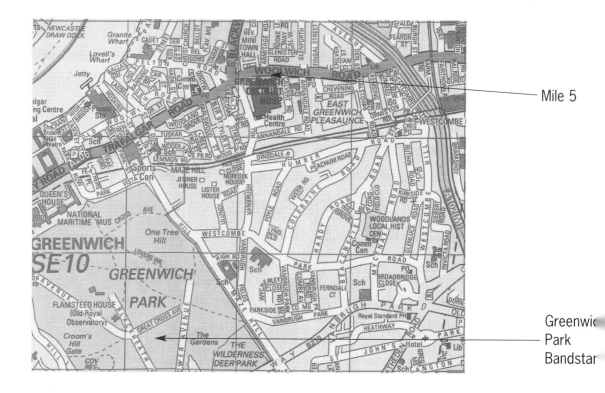

Mile 5

Greenwich
Park
Bandstand

MILE 18, East Ferry Rd (outside Millwall Pk)

Angela &
Meurig

ON YOUR MARKS...

Check out the website below for train times to Greenwich Park Station. You can walk very easily from the Greenwich Park Bandstand meeting point to the Blue and Green starts.

Visit www.railtrack.co.uk

or you can call national rail enquiries on 08457 48 49 50.

WHERE DO I START?

Numbers	Start	Start Time
150 – 1,149	Elite runners, BLUE / Blackheath	09:00
1,150 – 25,999	BLUE / Blackheath	09:30
26,000 – 47,499	RED / Greenwich Park	09:30
47,500 – 49,999	GREEN / Blackheath	09:30

Make sure you leave plenty of time to get to the start. All trains heading to Greenwich and Blackheath will be packed out and you might have quite a wait until you're able to get on one.

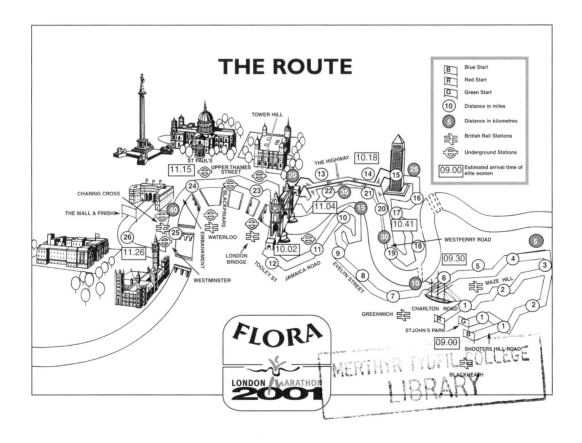

ROUTE PLANNER

Red Start: Charlton Way Vanbrugh Park

Mile
1 Charlton Way
2 Corner of Charlton Park and Little Heath

Blue Start: Shooters Hill Road

Mile
1 Shooters Hill Road
2 Charlton Park Lane

All Runners

Mile
 3 John Wilson Street
 4 Woolwich Church Street
 5 Woolwich Road
 6 Trafalgar Road (**10 km point**)
 7 Creek Street
 8 Evelyn Street
 9 Evelyn Street
10 Salter Road
11 Brunel Road
12 Tooley Street
13 Corner of East Smithfield Street
     and The Highway (**half way point**)
14 The Highway
15 Corner of West India Dock Road
     and Poplar High Street (**25 km point**)
16 Canary Wharf
17 Marsh Wall
18 East Ferry Road
19 West Ferry Road (**30 km point**)
20 West Ferry Road
21 Narrow Street
22 Thomas Moore Street
23 Lower Thames Street
24 Upper Thames Street
25 Victoria Embankment (**40 km point**)
26 Birdcage Walk
Finish The Mall

PACE GUIDE

Make sure you see your friends at as many points as possible by using the pace guide to work out when they will reach each mile point. The table shows six pace guides, from a 2 hour 30 minute finish to a five hour finish.

PACE GUIDE

1M	2M	3M	5km	4M	5M	6M	10km	Marathon
5:43	11:26	17.09	17:45	22:52	28:35	34:18	35:30	2:30:00
6:52	13:44	20:36	21:19	27:28	34:20	41:18	42:38	3:00:00
8:01	16:02	24:03	24:53	32:04	40:05	48:06	49:46	3:30:00
9:09	18:18	27:27	28:24	36:36	45:45	54:54	56:48	4:00:00
10:18	20:36	30:54	31:59	41:12	51:30	1:01:48	1:03:58	4:30:00
11:27	22:54	34:21	35:33	45:48	57:15	1:08:42	1:11:06	5:00:00

7M	8M	9M	15km	10M	11M	12M	Marathon
40:01	45:44	51:27	53:15	57:10	1:02:53	1:08:36	2:30:00
48:04	54:56	1:01:48	1:03:57	1:08:40	1:15:32	1:22:24	3:00:00
56:07	1:04:08	1:12:09	1:14:49	1:20:10	1:28:11	1:36:12	3:30:00
1:04:03	1:13:12	1:22:21	1:25:12	1:31:30	1:40:39	1:49:48	4:00:00
1:12:06	1:22:24	1:32:42	1:35:57	1:43:00	1:53:18	2:03:36	4:30:00
1:20:09	1:31:36	1:43:03	1:46:39	1:54:30	2:05:57	2:17:24	5:00:00

20km	133M	13.1M	14M	15M	25km	16M	Marathon
1:11:00	1:14:19	1:15:00	1:20:02	1:25:45	1:28:45	1:31:28	2:30:00
1:25:16	1:29:16	1:30:00	1:36:08	1:43:00	1:46:35	1:49:52	3:00:00
1:39:32	1:44:13	1:45:00	1:52:14	2:00:15	2:05:15	2:08:16	3:30:00
1:53:36	1:58:57	2:00:00	2:08:06	2:17:15	2:22:00	2:26:24	4:00:00
2:07:56	2:13:54	2:15:00	2:24:12	2:34:30	2:39:55	2:44:48	4:30:00
2:22:12	2:28:51	2:30:00	2:40:18	2:51:45	2:57:45	3:03:12	5:00:00

17M	18M	30km	19M	20M	21M	35kn	Marathon
1:37:11	1:42:54	1:46:30	1:48:37	1:54:20	2:00:03	2:04:15	2:30:00
1:56:44	2:03:36	2:07:54	2:10:28	2:17:20	2:24:12	2:29:13	3:00:00
2:16:17	2:24:18	2:29:38	2:32:19	2:40:20	2:48:21	2:54:21	3:30:00
2:35:33	2:44:42	2:50:54	2:53:51	3:03:00	3:12:09	3:18:48	4:00:00
2:55:06	3:05:24	3:11:54	33:25:42	3:26:00	3:36:18	3:43:53	4:30:00
3:14:39	3:26:06	3:33:18	3:37:33	3:49:00	4:00:27	4:08:51	5:00:00

22M	23M	24M	40km	25M	26M	Marathon
2:05:46	2:11:29	2:17:12	2:22:00	2:22:55	2:28:38	2:30:00
2:31:04	2:37:56	2:44:48	2:50:32	2:51:40	2:58:32	3:00:00
2:56:22	3:04:23	3:12:24	3:19:04	3:20:25	3:28:26	3:30:00
3:21:18	3:30:27	3:39:36	3:47:12	3:48:45	3:57:54	4:00:00
3:46:36	3:56:54	4:07:12	3:15:52	4:17:30	4:27:48	4:30:00
4:11:54	4:23:21	4:34:48	3:44:24	4:46:15	4:57:42	5:00:00

Pages 65–66 is from the 'Flora London Marathon 2000 Official Programme', The London Marathon Ltd.

TRANSPORT

If you choose to watch the Starts at Greenwich and Blackheath, a short jog or swift walk will take you to the six mile/10km points and the Cutty Sark.

Docklands Light Railway

With the opening of the Lewisham extension in November, the new DLR stations at Greenwich and Cutty Sark Gardens are close to the Start. Passengers can connect with DLR at Bank, Tower Gateway, Stratford, Canning Town and Canary Wharf Underground stations. For Kent passengers DLR also connects with Connex South Eastern at Lewisham and Greenwich in addition to the many bus routes which serve Lewisham. The first train from Bank and Lewisham will be at approximately 07.00am.

The new stations at Cutty Sark Gardens and Greenwich also give easy access to the Isle of Dogs, where there are ideal spots for viewing the race at Mudchute, Crossharbour, South Quay, Heron Quays, Canary Wharf and Poplar. All of these stations are adjacent to the Marathon route and the trains, on their elevated tracks, provide great vantage points. From these stations spectators can continue towards the Finish, either via Tower Gateway and then Tower Hill Station on the London Underground (District & Circle Lines) or via Bank and then transfer to London Underground.

Jubilee Line

New stations Canada Water and Bermondsey are close to the Marathon route. From London Bridge Station spectators can cross the river via London Bridge to see the runners at 23 miles. Canary Wharf Station on the Jubilee Line is also very convenient for spectators.

Passengers travelling back towards the Finish on the Jubilee Line should note that Westminster Station <u>may not</u> be open on Race Day this year. Check final instructions issued at registration for latest information.

The Greenwich Foot Tunnel will be closed southbound (ie: from the Isle of Dogs to Greenwich) from 10am until 12 noon on Marathon Day. A free DLR service will be available to passengers from Island Gardens to Cutty Sark only.

The East London Underground line (New Cross to Shoreditch) will provide an easy connection between Surrey Quays (just before the 9 mile point) and Shadwell – 5 minutes from The Highway (14 and 21 miles).

From Shadwell you can transfer to the DLR and either go east to any of the stations open on the Isle of Dogs section of the route or west to Tower Hill. From Tower Hill you can catch the runners between 22 and 23 miles (St Katharine's Dock or The Tower although this area does become very crowded) or continue onward via London Underground to The Embankment and catch the runners as they pass along Victoria Embankment. Alternatively, go direct to Charing Cross and meet your friends or relatives at the designated repatriation areas in Horse Guards Road.

3

KEY SKILLS COMMUNICATION LEVEL 3: LANGUAGE

WHAT YOU MUST DO

C3.1a
Contribute to a group discussion about a complex subject.

C3.1b
Make a presentation about a complex subject using at least one image to illustrate complex points.

C3.2
Read and synthesise information from two extended documents about a complex subject.

One of these documents should include at least one image.

C3.3
Write two different types of documents about complex subjects.

One piece of writing should be an extended document and include at least one image.

A LEVEL ENGLISH LANGUAGE TASK

The following task will address **C3.1a**, **C3.1b**, **C3.2** and one section of **C3.3**.

Revision Exercise

In groups of four.

Your task is to provide a 15 minute revision session for the whole class on any of the topics you have studied over the past 18 months. You must make this lively and entertaining but your main purpose is to be informative. In addition, you are asked to produce a revision aid which can be used by the class. Try to use diagrams and pictures or an unusual format for your revision aid.

Why?

Evidence has shown that we need to activate all our senses if we are to revise properly. We remember twenty per cent of what we read, thirty per cent of what we hear, forty per cent of what we see, fifty per cent of what we say, sixty per cent of what we do, **but ninety per cent of what we read, hear, see, say and do**.

The very best way to check if you have really understood something is to try to teach it to someone else. By planning a revision session on a topic on which you will be examined, you will have the double benefit of helping yourself to understand that topic and helping others to understand it too.

This exercise will sharpen up your case study skills such as:

- script writing

- presenting information to an audience

- audience awareness techniques

- preparation of images

- introduction of images into a written text

- selection of data

- varying the way information is presented

- sequencing

- precis.

This exercise will also fulfil the requirements of the Key Skill Unit Communication **C3.1a**, **C3.1b** and **C3.2**, if you keep evidence of all the procedures you follow to complete this task. By producing a script you will also have one document to contribute to **C3.3**.

The task falls into two parts. **Part 1** is the preparation and selection of the material. **Part 2** is the actual presentation to the class.

Part 1 The Preparation

In groups

Work with at least two other people and make the following decisions.

1   Which area of the course do you think you would like to use for your revision session?

Remember, each member of the group will have to make a three to four minute presentation to the class. You need to choose your topic carefully as every member of the group has to feel confident about addressing one particular area of the chosen topic. The overall presentation will take about 15 minutes if you are in a group of four.

As an example, your group might choose to present a revision session on Language and Power. One speaker might choose to discuss the way language can be used by social groups to gain power, another might like to examine language structures which give the speaker power and another might want to discuss jargon and metalanguage. A different member of the group might want to look at written texts to see how we can use our knowledge of language and power when we do a stylistic analysis.

You can see from this example that although you are all contributing to the same topic, you are all developing completely different presentations.

2   The next stage of this task is for the group to consider the following questions. What is the best sequence for your material? Who will speak first? How will the sections link together? You need to make these decisions within your group.

3   Each speaker must use at least one image. This can be a picture or a chart or a brainstorming diagram or anything which will help your audience to understand the information. You can provide a handout for your audience too. You need to have this planned well in advance so that OHP transparencies and handouts can be reproduced for you.

Your group planning meetings will contribute to the Key Skills Award. You have to:

* make clear and relevant contributions in a way that suits your purpose and situation

* listen and respond sensitively to others, develop points and ideas, and

* create opportunities for others to contribute where appropriate.

Part of your discussion might be recorded to use as evidence for the Key Skills Award.

When you have decided on your topic area you need to create your script. This is where you will practise your case study skills. The script, together with any images you use, will contribute to your portfolio for **C3.2** and **C3.3**, the written element of your Key Skills Award in Communication. It is not intended that you simply read out your speech when you give your revision session. You can make yourself a set of cue cards but you cannot read your text word for word. Your teacher might video your spoken presentation and you might even want to compare your spoken presentation with your written script. This would enable you to study the differences between spoken and written text and you will see how a speech works when it is presented to an audience rather than just being written on paper. This should help make you all expert speech writers and make you aware of how you can keep your audience interested in what you are saying.

When all the group members have chosen their areas of study you are ready to move on to the preparation of materials. You need to tackle this part of the exercise in the same way that you would tackle a case study. This only difference is that instead of the examiner choosing the information for you to study and reproduce in another format, you will be selecting the material yourself.

Look at the notes you have made on the topic of your choice. Is there sufficient there for you to develop the notes into a three minute talk?

Remember you have to provide an image. It would be really useful if you could provide a revision sheet in an unusual format to give to the class. Use pictures, charts, tables – anything that you think will make the information easy to retain. Some example sheets have been included to help you.

Part 2 The Presentation

Now that you have written your script, designed your revision aid (your image), and produced your cue cards, the final step is to present your revision session to the group.

Make sure that you have all the equipment you need. It would be helpful if your revision aid was of the type that would fit on to a piece of A4 or A3 paper so that it can be photocopied and handed out at the beginning of your presentation. **Please make sure your revision aid is not an essay**.

You might like to spend some time talking about your revision sheet and discussing how it might be used.

Don't forget to keep all your notes and drafts as they will be needed for evidence that you have fulfilled the key skills requirements of this exercise. Keep them safely in your portfolio. Remember to look at the images produced by other A Level students that have been supplied. They will give you some ideas to think about.

FEATURES OF MALE AND FEMALE SPEECH REVISION AID (EXAMPLE)

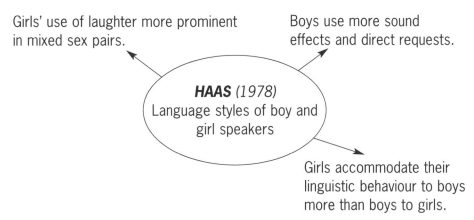

Girls' use of laughter more prominent in mixed sex pairs.

Boys use more sound effects and direct requests.

HAAS *(1978)*
Language styles of boy and girl speakers

Girls accommodate their linguistic behaviour to boys more than boys to girls.

Goodwin (1990)

Observed girls and boys playing in a Philadelphia street.

FINDINGS	EXAMPLE
Boys use explicit commands	*'Gimmie the pliers'* *'Get off my steps'*
Girls tend to use mitigated directives	*Let's go round to Sue & Sally's'* *Let's ask her "do you have any bottles?"*
Girls tend to use modal auxiliaries	*Would, could, should, may, can, must, might, will*
The form *'let's'* is hardly ever used by boys	

Robin Lakoff

Research into lexis.

- Women use more empty adjectives e.g. sweet, lovely, gorgeous.

- Women use more intensifiers in speech e.g. so, very, really, absolutely.

- Women have more specialist vocabularies in some areas e.g. colour terms – a man may say a colour is purple while a woman would call it amethyst.

Lakoff, Coates, Holmes & Others

Various linguistic studies by these people have shown that:

- Woman are more likely to use hedges in speech e.g. sort of, kind of.

- Women are more likely to use politeness forms e.g. do you think you could, would you mind.

- Women are more likely to use questioning intonation in declarative compliments particularly from one woman to another.

- Women are more likely to use tag questions e.g. isn't it, aren't we.

CLASSROOM LANGUAGE (EXAMPLE)

DEBORAH TANNEN

- Boys got maximum individual attention from their teacher.

- Girls were praised for their looks.

- Girls gave their speaking power away to boys.

- Boys took up the 'verbal space' during class discussions.

AN AMERICAN STUDY

- Boys were 8 times more likely to call out in class than girls.

- Even though boys took up more of the 'speaking space', girls were found to be more talkative and fluent. However, this report did not specify whether this was in the playground or the classroom.

JENNY CHESHIRE

- Girls were more inclined to shift their language style. They used more standard forms in the classroom than the playground.

- Boys tended to use more non-standard forms in class as a way of rebelling against the teacher.

CHECKLIST
PRE C20TH LANGUAGE DEVICES (EXAMPLE)

- The Magic 'e'
  This makes any vowel that is followed by the combination of consonant + e alter its pronunciation. E.g. mad becomes made.

- Fenetick spelying (phonetic spelling)
  People spelt phonetically (how the word sounded) as there was no dictionary until 1755. E.g. 'unmixed' was often spelt 'unmixt', as this was how the word was pronounced. Accent and dialect may have influenced how words were spelt.

- 'Y' and 'I' interchange
  As both of these letters can form the same sound, people often put an 'i' in place of a 'y', and vice versa.

- Double vowels/consonants
  Double vowels and consonants were often used purely due to phonetic spelling.

- Silent letters
  Used by the Bishop of Cambridge, who thought that this would add prestige to the English language. He borrowed Latin spellings that gave us the 'b' in debt and the 's' in island.

- Sentence length
  Look out for long sentences as these were characteristic of pre-C20th texts.

- 'U' and 'V'
  'U' and 'V' are often interchangeable due to the style of printing press that was used at this time.

- Formality
  Writing was very formal at this time, even between family members.

- Archaisms
  Look for words that aren't used in modern language or words that have changed their meaning. E.g. wherein, doth.

TIMELINE – ENGLISH LANGUAGE CHANGE

449 (AD) — Angles, Saxons and Jutes start to migrate from Europe. Latin – rich people's language, Celtish – poor people's language.

Vikings begin to migrate, bringing Old Norse. Need for communication prompted change. — **700**

1066 — Normans invade England. French is the language of power.

Middle English – French and English mixed. — **1150**

1349 — English re-instated as teaching medium in schools.

French forbidden in law courts because ordinary people don't understand. — **1362**

1450 — The start of The Great Vowel Shift. Pronunciation moved away from written words.

Caxton began to use the printing press. Printing encouraged standardisation. Renaissance period results in many borrowed words. — **1476**

1582 — Richard Mulcaster wrote *Elementarie*.

Vowels now pronounced differently. — **1600**

1755 — Dr Samuel Johnson's dictionary published. Spelling becomes standardised in England.

Noah Webster's American dictionary published. Centre (E), center (A); colour (E), color (A); defence (E), defense (A). — **1828**

1870 — Education introduced for all children, resulting in mass literacy.

Large number of changes in English Language. — **1900**

2000 — Keep moving forward?

MINI DATA INVESTIGATION

The following task will allow students to achieve **C3.1a**, **C3.1b**, **C3.2**, **C3.3**. Data included in this book is ideal for the purposes of a mini investigation but teachers can use alternative data or encourage students to collect their own. This would ideally be an AS year task, used as an introduction to the data collection and analysis process.

Students should be in groups of four to six. Each student will need a copy of the data and the instruction sheet. You might also want to provide them with OHP acetates and any other presentation materials they may need.

Students should keep copies of their presentational material and their reports for their portfolio.

If students need to fulfil the requirements of IT Key Skills they should be encouraged to word process all their presentation materials and include computer-generated images.

We have included a selection of personal advertisements reproduced from the *Guardian*. You might want to find your own advertisements. Other suggested sources are the *Guardian* (Saturday), *Private Eye,* local newspaper, Teletext or the Internet.

INVESTIGATION OF DATA

Mini Investigation

Aim
The purpose of this task is to familiarise you with the principles of investigative technique and to allow you to explore the many ways in which data can be analysed. It will also show you the value of working with others when considering your ideas about language and how explaining your thoughts to others helps you to learn more about the investigation process.

Equipment needed
You will need the data provided, a team of keen linguists, paper, pens, flip chart, OHP acetates, any other presentation materials you can find, presentation score sheets (optional)

Method
- Read the data provided. Make your own initial note about what it is and why it might be important from a language point of view.

- In your team, discuss your observations and list all the possible areas of investigation you can think of.

- Discuss which areas of investigation might prove most interesting. As a team decide which line of investigation you will pursue.

- Decide which features of language will tell you more about your chosen line of investigation; for example, the use of nouns, adjectives, semantic fields, rhyme and so on. These features will become your classifications.

- Choose four classifications and divide them between your team.

- Everyone should now extract or list all the data relating to their classification. Remember someone should also count the number of items of data so you can calculate percentages later!

- Now for the analysis. Look at your classifications closely. Are there any patterns emerging? Does anything strike you as unusual? Can you quantify your findings (in other words turn them into helpful charts, diagrams or graphs).

- Turn your findings into a visual aid that will explain them to the rest of the class.

- Compare what individual members of the team have found. What do the different classifications tell you about the team's line of enquiry?

- Draw your team conclusions and turn them into a visual aid.

- Plan how you will present these findings to the rest of the class.

- Make sure everyone is included in the presentation. You should plan for your presentation to last between 10 and 15 minutes.

- Write up your findings individually as a report.

SOULMATES

The Guardian

**Women
seeking men**
*London, South East
& South West*

● **Interesting Aquarius**
Slim, attract, bubbly, profess, petite, blue-eyed blonde, **38**, into film, eating in & out, theatre, travel & music. Seeks soulmate, sim ints, for f/ship+. Herts.

● **Who Cares Wins**
Attract, educ lady **68**, enjoys adaptable ints, WLTM sim gentleman to spend quality time together. So take the plunge. Kent/Ldn.

● **Modern Romance**
Curvaceous F **32**, 5', works in publishing, likes laughs, walks in the parks. Seeks witty, romantic M, for f/ship+. Ldn.

● **Brighton Belle**
Good-looking, slim, blue-eyed F **38**, GSOH, interested in the Zodiac, good conversation, reading, & music. WLTM intellig M for friendship, perhaps r/ship. Brighton.

● **Mutual TLC**
Tall, slim F **50**, (25 in mind & body), enjoys travel, walks, music & laughter. Seeks warm, cheerful n/s M with whom to age disgracefully. Herts.

● **Stop Here –
   New Message!**
Golden-maned F **22**, shy art history grad, 5'10, n/s, passion for human rights, travel, culture, sport & singing. WLTM outgoing, taller kind man. Cambridge.

● **Seeking Patrick**
I lost your number, I need to talk to you again, pls call. Billie.

● **Rice & Peace**
Attract slim F **36**, 5'7, into travel, music, yoga. Seeks creative, confident, tall, slim W. Indian M for poss r/ship. Brighton.

● **Write On**
Attract, blonde blue-eyed F **35**, 5'6, charity worker, into gigs, dancing, parties, galleries, bars & writing. Seeks TDH M 33–45, for loving r/ship. Ldn.

● **Just Believe**
Curvaceous, sometimes feisty, attract F. Seeks tall, black profess M for football, f/ship, dinner, dirty dancing, maybe more. Ldn.

● **Perhaps Perhaps
   Perhaps**
Free-spirited, warm, indpt F. Seeks lively, together, profess M for f/ship & maybe more. Brighton.

● **Light Thoughtful F**
Optimistic, well-travelled, n/s profess F **58**, WLTM M with young outlook & great SOH for? Ldn.

● **Special Offer**
Unconventional, sorted F **34**, likes chatting, music & adventures. Seeks M 30–40ish to make her laugh out loud. Bristol.

● **Blonde Ambition**
Sexy but size 16 F **35**, into film. Seeks kind, intellig M 30–50, for ... Ldn.

● **Veg F**
Happy, friendly, enjoys life, into eating out, disco dancing & arts. Seeks M 30s, with own life. Brighton.

● **Current Attraction**
Woman, **39**, slimish, enjoys modern music, contemporary art, loves animals. Wants to spend some time with a relaxed interesting man. Ldn.

● **Cuddly & Bubbly**
Attract blonde F, late **40**s, into theatre, cinema, socialising. Seeks tall, intellig gentle M, GSOH, for f/ship or r/ship. Essex.

● **Serious & Fun**
Honest, kind, indpt F **40**s, veg, n/s, enjoys walking, good food, talking with friends. Seeks compatible M. Ldn.

● **Leggy & Loyal**
Slim brunette F, languishing in beautiful Suffolk village. Seeks tall, imaginative, hunky, passionate n/s M 40–50, for love & f/ship. Suffolk.

● **Come Prom With Me**
Intellig, passionate, attract F **40**s, profess. Seeks (preferably) younger M for non-heavy r/ship. Walking, wine, classical music ... surprises an advantage. Ldn.

● **Active Attract**
F **35**, loves cycling, walking, skiing, occasionally jumping out of aeroplanes. Seeks M excited by life. Bristol.

● **Full Of Fun**
Two girls **24** & **33**, with plenty of front. Seek Robbie Williams × two, 28–35 for nights out, GSOH more important than ability to sing. Ldn.

● **Wild At Heart**
Attract F brunette **29**, loves film, reading & eating out. Seeks tall, unpretentious bloke, 29–35, with sharp wit. Middx.

● **Forever Optimistic**
Attract, slim F, mid **40**s, GSOH, loves art, music, walking & travel. Seeks n/s, youthful M 40s. Ldn.

● **Trans-Personal Connection**
Young-looking, attract profess F **43**, into personal growth & fitness. WLTM M therapist, or sim, who loves Jesus, 38–50. Ldn.

● **Yoko Seeks
   Working Class Hero**
For instant Karma & world peace. Mixed-race social science grad, **36**, seeks soulmate for bed-ins, bag-ism & lots of deep stuff. Ldn.

● **Non-traditional Punjabi**
Sought by attract socialite into friends & family. Needs to be cherished by intellig M 35–40, who can multi-task. Ldn.

● **Make Me Laugh**
Slightly bent & twisted F **33**. Seeks witty, intellig M, GSOH, for laughs & adventure in Ldn.

● **Yes Pls**
F **34**, finding greatest pleasure in small things, requires reflective, curious, sorted, funny M 30s, good heart, for gleaming future. Ldn.

● **No Fun-damentalists**
Fun-loving, attract, petite Asian-Muslim F **40**, flexible about religion, likes walks, travel & eating out. Seeks caring, honest, easy-going M, GSOH. Ldn.

● **Free Spirited**
Intellig, creative F, with very own dot com. Seeks bright, idiosyncratic M with good ideas, 38–48. Ldn.

● **Double Entendre**
Two intellig, friendly F's, GSOH, enjoy home-cooking & adventurous travel. Seek two cheerful chaps for f/ship & poss r/ship. Ldn.

Men
seeking women
London, South East
& South West

Dream Lover
Dream of a good home, prospects? Tall, slim, assertive, solvent white M **46**, seeks younger white F. No disco flyer, only lover, pls. Ldn.

Paradise Cove
Live your fantasies on my private beach. V. fit, slim, **40**s M, artistic outdoor type. WLTM F 30–50, for seaside fun & explorations. Cornwall/London.

From Shanghai With Love
Profess Chinese M **35**, into theatre, cinema & fast cars. Seeks attract, happy, romantic F. Ldn.

Let's Make History
Kind, attract, hazel-eyed M **38**, 6′1, into arts, history, music, country pubs. Seeks tall, slim F 30s, for fun, poss r/ship. Ldn.

Designer For Life
Slim, dark-haired M **38**, 5′11, GSOH, designer, likes restaurants, theatre, film & gigs. Seeks non-materialistic F 30–40, to share ints. Ldn.

Perfect Fit
Attract, dark-haired M, young **38**, 5′7, GSOH, likes music, film, fitness, walks, cycling, travel & restaurants. Seeks attract F 30s, sim ints. Ldn.

Times Out
Tall profess M **29**, likes good times & socialising. WLTM F 20–30, for fun & f/ship. Ldn.

Homer Lone
Bespectacled, balding M **34**, 6′2, civil servant, likes eating out, Simpsons, jam. Seeks F for ace times & more. Ldn.

Shared Fun
Unattached, profess M **51**, seeking long-term f/ship leading to committed r/ship with caring F. Berks.

Vidal Statistics
Mousy-haired M **32**, 6′, Guardian stereotype, satirical SOH, film & lit snob, into American fiction & South American travel. Seeks F for f/ship+. Ldn.

Candle You Call Me
Tall, sharp-witted, interesting, good-looking M **32**. Seeks F for candle-lit dinners & maybe more. Essex.

For Starters
Shy, slim M **40**, GSOH, likes theatre, cinema, music, reading, cooking, restaurants & pubs. Seeks F 30–40 to bring out the best in him. Surrey.

Strong In-tention
Attract M **34**, 5′10, civil engineer, likes music, socialising, amateur dramatics & reading. Seeks F, sim ints, for f/ship+. Ldn.

Let's Play House
Slim n/s M **39**, 5′11, likes cinema, theatre, opera, ballet. Seeks special F 26–40, sim ints, for f/ship, poss r/ship. Ldn.

Oh What A Knight!
Profess white M **29**, 6′1, sporty & chivalrous, enjoys wild nights out, music, reading. Seeks intellig black F for companionship+. Ldn.

Etch-a-sketch
Relaxed n/s M **50**, 5′11, GSOH, likes painting, cinema, walking, gardening, cooking. Seeks F to see his etchings. Ldn.

The Graduate 2
28 yo 6′2 M, seeks Anne Bancroft for good times. Bristol.

Half-way To ATwoway
Unpredictable, inconsistent h'some M, approaching **30**, privy to post-rock & afternoon naps. Seeks sim F 28–35. Brighton.

Articulate Tactile & Reliable
M **37**. Seeks independent F to share l'term r/ship, including films, dining, pubs, countryside, adventures & fun. Bristol.

Watcher In Waiting Willow?
Tall, sardonic M grad, **24**, pop culture vulture. Seeks truly remarkable Ldn F for coffee, Catullus, Copeland & stuff. Credible? Ldn.

Earthy Ideas Man
5′10, **45**, slimish, darkish, loves landscape, arts, history, nearly DIY. Seeks warm, feminine, tomboy for wrestling, relaxation & realignment. Brighton.

Future Imperfect
Warm-hearted, humorous, profess, playful M **49**, enjoys good food, R4, ordinary things. Seeks attract, tolerant, imperfect F. Ldn.

One Man In A Boat
Likes music, cycling, cooking, canoeing & Jerome K Jerome. Seeks intellig, curvaceous, fun-loving, considerate F 30–40. Ldn.

Ldn Gent 31
Tactile, romantic, warm-hearted & spontaneous. Seeks older lady to fall in love with.

Yes – The Future
Tall, athletic, profess white bloke, GSOH. WLTM small, curvy black F 25–35, for solid, loyal r/ship. Ldn.

West Of Eden
Tall, slim, fit grad guy, **40**s. Seeks F 19–31, laid-back profess or student, for good times. Oxon.

The Eddie Izzard Of The Home Counties
Whimsical artist with eclectic tastes, hoping to meet like-minded F. Oxon.

Consider This
Intellig, attract, genuine M **37**, profess, likes film, music, art, design & travel. WLTM sim, attract F for f/ship & r/ship. Ldn.

The Tall Guy
M **36**, tall, slim, easy-going, loves music, galleries, cinema, etc. Seeks older F 45–55, to share love & laughter. Ldn/SE.

Soulful Guy
H'some M **45**, loves music arts, walking & travel. WLTM enthusiastic, sensuous F. Brighton.

Lazing & Loving
Young black M **36**, loves music, dancing, clubbing, movies, current affairs. Seeks black/mixed race F 30–35, to share fun times. Ldn.

Fireside Favourite
Lady, 30–50, who enjoys wearing polo-neck sweaters, knitting, cooking & log fires. Sought by attract, big, blue-eyed M **40**. Soton.

Looking For A Hottie
Attract, intellig, romantic, successful American, **37**, GSOH, seeks slim, attract F 24–34, for cinema, dining, travel & fun in Ldn.

Bring Me Life!
Warm-hearted, grad, **22**, ambitious for life not work. WLTM F 20–24, for fun, maybe more. Ldn.

Soulmates Are Us
Decent M **29**, seeks slim, sincere, fun-loving F 18–25, for fun, love, romance & great laughs. Ldn.

Foreign Travel
Journalist-photog, seeks guest/travel mate. 21–35, ints in visiting exciting places world-wide. No steady job ties. Able to travel regularly. Ldn.

TDH Engineer
M **33**, likes eating out, cooking at home, beers & occasional theatre. WLTM F for sim or something totally different. Ldn.

KEY SKILLS COMMUNICATION LEVEL 3: LITERATURE

WHAT YOU MUST DO:

C3.1a
Contribute to a group discussion about a complex subject.

C3.1b
Make a presentation about a complex subject using at least one image to illustrate complex points.

C3.2
Read and synthesise information from two extended documents about a complex subject.

One of these documents should include at least one image.

C3.3
Write two different types of documents about complex subjects.

One piece of writing should be an extended document and include at least one image.

A LEVEL ENGLISH LITERATURE TASK

Oral Presentation

The following task will address **C3.1a**, **C3.1b**, **C3.2**. If you choose to write up your script you will also fulfil the requirements of one section of **C3.3**.

Revision Exercise

In groups of four.
Your task is to provide a 15 minute revision session for the whole class on any of the texts you have studied over the past few months. You must make this lively and entertaining but your main purpose is to be informative. In addition, you are asked to produce a revision aid which can be used by the class. Try to use diagrams and pictures or an unusual format for your revision aid.

Why?

Evidence has shown that we need to activate all our senses if we are to revise properly. We remember twenty per cent of what we read, thirty per cent of what we hear, forty per cent of what we see, fifty per cent of what we say, sixty per cent of what we do, **but ninety per cent of what we read, hear, see, say and do**.

The very best way to check if you have really understood something is to try to teach it to someone else. By planning a revision session on a topic on which you will be examined, you will have the double benefit of helping yourself to understand that topic and helping others to understand it too.

This exercise will also fulfil the requirements of the Key Skills Communication **C3.1a**, **C3.1b** and **C3.2** if you keep evidence of all the procedures you follow to complete this task. If you choose to produce a scripted talk, you can hand it in for assessment so you will also have one document to contribute to **C3.3**.

The task falls into two parts. **Part 1** is the preparation and selection of the material. **Part 2** is the actual presentation to the class.

Part 1 The Preparation

In groups

Work with at least two other people and make the following decisions.

1   Which of the set texts would your group like to concentrate on for your revision session?

Remember that each member of the group will have to make a three to four minute presentation to the class. Once you have chosen your text, you need to focus on a specific area for revision. You cannot cover the whole text in the time you have available. The overall presentation will take about 15 minutes if you are in a group of four.

You could choose to focus on a particular theme or to look at the roles of the major characters. You might like to focus on stylistic features or you might want to discuss the context in which the text was written. You could give information about the author or about the genre or discuss what the critics have said about the novel, play or poems that you are studying.

As an example, your group might choose to present a revision session on the examination text *Six Women Poets*. Your group decides to focus on the work of one poet, but you each choose a different area to present to the class. TWO of you might speak about the themes you have found, giving quotations to reinforce your points. Another person in the group might like to point out the stylistic devices of the poetry and the fourth member of the group might like to give some background details about the poet to set the texts in context.

You can see from this example that although you are all contributing to the same topic, you are all developing completely different presentations.

2   The next stage of this task is for the group to consider the following questions. What is the best sequence for your material? Who will speak first? How will the sections link together? You need to make these decisions within your group.

3   Each speaker must use at least one image. This can be a picture or a chart or a collage or a quotations sheet with picture prompts or **anything** which will help your audience to understand the information. One has been provided

as an illustration. You can provide a handout for your audience too. You need to have this planned well in advance so that OHP transparencies and handouts can be reproduced for you.

Your group planning meetings will contribute to the Key Skills Award. You have to:

- make clear and relevant contributions in a way that suits your purpose and situation

- listen and respond sensitively to others, develop points and ideas, and

- create opportunities for others to contribute where appropriate.

Part of your discussion might be recorded to use as evidence for the Key Skills Award.

When you have decided on your topic area you need to create your script. The script, together with any images you use, will contribute to your portfolio for **C3.2** and **C3.3**, the written element of your Key Skills Award in Communication. It is not intended that you simply read out your speech when you give your revision session. You can make yourself a set of cue cards but you cannot read your text word for word.

When all the group members have chosen what they are going to do, you are ready to move on to the next stage – the preparation of your materials.

Remember you have to provide an image. It would be really useful if you could provide a revision sheet in an unusual format to give to the class. Use pictures, charts, tables – anything that you think will make the information easy to retain.

Part 2 The Presentation.

Now that you have written your script, designed your revision aid (your image), and produced your cue cards, the final step is to present your revision session to the group.

Before you begin your presentation you must make sure that you have all the equipment you need. It would be helpful if your revision aid was of the type that would fit on to a piece of A4 or A3 paper, so that it can be photocopied and handed out at the beginning of your presentation. We have included some revision aids that students from a Sixth Form College in Nottingham have prepared. They might give you some ideas to use when you make your own sheet. **Please make sure your revision aid is not an essay.**

You might like to spend some time talking about your revision sheet and discussing how it might be used.

Don't forget to keep all your notes and drafts as they will be needed for evidence that you have fulfilled the key skills requirements of this exercise. Keep them safely in your portfolio.

THORNFIELD

I am hard and tough as an Indian rubber ball.

Now that you think me disqualified to become your husband, you recoil from my touch as if I were some toad or a

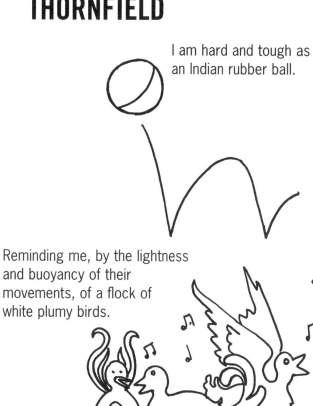

Reminding me, by the lightness and buoyancy of their movements, of a flock of white plumy birds.

A Christmas frost had come at Midsummer; a white December storm had whirled over June.

The tinkle of the bell [had] as much significance as their laugh.

I should have had one vital struggle with two tigers – jealousy and despair.

Don't long for poison – don't turn out a downright Eve on my hands!

MOORHOUSE

Whereas I am hot, and fire dissolves ice.

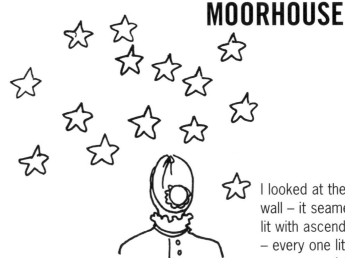

I looked at the blank wall – it seamed a sky lit with ascending stars – every one lit me to a purpose or delight.

Our natures dovetailed – ritual affection of the strangest kind was the result.

His look was not, indeed, of a lover beholding his mistress, but it was that … of a guardian angel watching the soul for which he is responsible.

The pillow was burning, there is an asp in the garland; the wine has a bitter taste.

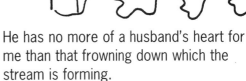

He has no more of a husband's heart for me than that frowning down which the stream is forming.

Serene inward feelings bloom and bud under the ray.

'Down superstition' I commented, as that spectre rose up in black by the black yew at the gate.

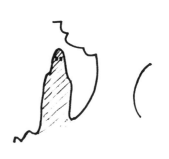

A LEVEL ENGLISH LANGUAGE AND LITERATURE TASK

THE LANGUAGE OF LITERATURE

The following task will allow students to achieve **C3.1a, C3.1b, C3.2, C3.3**. Most specifications require students to examine language features in comparative texts. This task can be adapted to suit the texts you are studying. For example, for the AQA specification B you could use *Alice in Wonderland* by Lewis Carroll and *The BFG* by Roald Dahl, as the basis for a study of language in children's literature.

Students should work in teams of four and have already read the texts to be examined. This task is suited to work in either the AS or A2 year. Each student will require a copy of the texts, plenty of materials to create visual aids, for example: posters, collages and charts, and a copy of the student instruction sheet.

Opportunities for using IT in the creation of presentation materials exist.

Students should keep copies of their presentational material and their written reports as portfolio evidence.

THE LANGUAGE OF LITERATURE

Aim:
During this task you will explore how different writers use language to achieve their purposes. You will see how different language features work within texts.

Equipment needed:
You will need – your copies of the texts you are studying, paper, pens, OHP, flip chart, a keen team of four literary critics.

Method:
- In your team discuss the key language features that you have observed in the texts. Do the writers use a lot of dialogue, metaphor, description, humour, complex vocabulary, unusual sentence structure and so on?

- Decide which features you find most interesting. Share your ideas with the class. Each team should then choose a different area to explore.

- As a team discuss the importance of your chosen topic. What might it tell you about the writer's intentions or the purposes of the text?

- Brainstorm the language features that you might examine within your topic. For example: grammar (verbs and tenses?), imagery (simple, complex, extended), world play (puns, connotations, euphemism), gender (descriptions of men or women, dialogue used by men or women).

- When you have a list of features divide them between the members of your team. Each team member should then look for examples of their feature in the texts. Draw up two lists, one of each text.

- When you have extracted a substantial number of examples, compare your lists. What are the differences or similarities? What do these examples reveal about the writer's style and purpose? Make notes.

- As a team, pool your findings. Are there any patterns starting to emerge? Can you start to draw conclusions about the differences or similarities? Do they tell you anything about the gender, age, race, historical context, social concerns of the writers?

- You now need to prepare a ten minute presentation of your findings to explain them to the rest of the class. You should use charts, images, pictures, tables and diagrams to illustrate your points and provide evidence for your conclusions.

- When each team has completed their presentation, have a class discussion to compare what each research topic has revealed.

- Write up your findings as a report.

SPEECH <u>AND</u> DRAMA

The following task will allow students to achieve **C3.1a**, **C3.1b**, **C3.2**, **C3.3**. All specifications require students to compare the language of scripts to the features of everyday speech. In this task students will put what they have learned about the features of speech into practice, whilst exploring the meaning of dramatic text. This activity can be used with any prescribed drama text. Students should keep copies of their new scripts and their written accounts as evidence for their portfolios.

Students will need copies of the drama text they are studying, a copy of the student instruction sheet, pens, paper and some space. A video camera will also be required.

SPEECH AND DRAMA

Aim:
The aim of this task is to explore the meaning of an extract from the play you are studying and to see how the writer has used language to express this meaning. You will also be comparing the language features of real speech to the language features of a dramatic text.

Equipment needed:
You will need: A copy of the drama text you are studying, pens, paper, space, a team of writers, actors and directors.

Method:
- Choose what your team considers to be two key scenes from the play.

- Re-read the scenes as a team and brainstorm the important themes, motivations, emotions and events that are portrayed.

- On a piece of paper, make a brief personality sketch of each character involved. (For example, Othello: black male, powerful, employed, in love, jealous.)

- List the emotions and motivations displayed in each scene (For example, anger, happiness, greed, to hurt the other person, to make friends.)

- Take your lists and character sketches and find yourself a space. Give each member of the team a character. If there are more team members than characters, double up.

- Take a few minutes to think about your characters qualities, what they want and what they feel.

- Stand in pairs facing each other. Take it in turns to talk to your partner in the role of the character you have been given. Use modern language and modern situations. (For example, Macbeth could be an angry gang leader who wants to steal his father's money.) Remember this is NOT the character from the play but the character you have sketched on paper.

- When you have begun to understand the new character you have created, it is time to start writing.

- As a team write a scene from a play, in modern English, that includes the characters and events that you have identified.

- When you have written the scene, rehearse it with your team.

- Present your new drama text to the rest of the class. Give a copy of the script to every member of the class.

- Your teacher will video your performance.

- Write an account of the process and compare your new script to the original text.

A LEVEL LANGUAGE/LANGUAGE AND LITERATURE TASK

ORIGINAL WRITING

The following task will allow students to achieve **C3.1a**, **C3.1b**, **C3.2**, **C3.3**. The task takes one aspect of original writing – writing to inform – as its focus. This is a good task for using IT as students will be designing their own web page. Students with enough expertise could do this as a web based project.

Students should work individually, although discussion of topics should initially be done in groups. The final piece can easily be used as a piece of original writing coursework.

Students will need: access to reference books about the English Language or Literary texts they are studying, access to the internet or to copies of web pages to use as models.

ORIGINAL WRITING

The English Web Page

Aim:
The aim of this task is to allow you to research a topic of your choice from your course. You will produce a piece of original writing that you can use as coursework or as a revision aid. You will learn about writing to inform.

Equipment:
You will need: reference books, access to the internet, copies of web pages, illustrations, diagrams or charts.

Method:

- In groups, discuss topics from your course that interest you. Brainstorm a list of topics that you think might make a good subject for a web page. Topics might include: Language and Gender, Dialect, Shakespeare's Theatre, Biographies of Writers.

- Each member of the group should choose a topic that they are going to research.

- Individually, use all the resources that are available to you to research your topic. You should use the internet, the library, periodicals, newspapers and so on. You must not rely on your class notes.

- Make notes on the source material you have used.

- Once you have enough material, start to think about how you could use this information to make a simple web page for A level students.

- Using the internet, or copies of web pages, as your model identify the key features of this sort of text. Think about the vocabulary you might use and how you could make your text as lively as possible.

- Write the text for your web page, remember it must be informative as well as entertaining. Your completed text should be between 1,000 and 1,500 words in total. This may mean that you have to have more than one page on your site.

- Once your text is complete, think about layout: headings, white space, length of paragraphs, hyper links and so on.

- Plan your page. It must include at least one image. This could be a chart, illustration, diagram or a table.

- Either on paper, or on a PC, create your page. For the purposes of this task it does not have to be an actual web page but should look like one!

- When everyone has completed a web page you can put them together on the college network or as a booklet for revision purposes.

4

EXEMPLAR TEST 1

LEVEL	PAPER	
Key skills – Level 3	Communication	**DOMESTIC VIOLENCE**

WHAT YOU NEED:

- a resource document booklet
- this task booklet
- paper
- pens with black or blue ink.

THERE ARE TWO PARTS TO THIS PAPER:

Part 1 – Short answer questions (25 marks)

Part 2 – Extended answer questions (25 marks)

ADDITIONAL AIDS

- dictionaries may not be used.

TIME ALLOWED – 1 HOUR 30 MINUTES. THIS INCLUDES READING TIME.

To complete this activity successfully you will need to:

- read the information supplied in the task booklet and the resource booklet
- complete both parts of the paper

INSTRUCTIONS TO CANDIDATES

- Write your personal details at the top of your first sheet of paper.
- Do not open this task booklet until you are told to do so by the supervisor.
- Read each question carefully and attempt all questions.
- Write in black or blue ink only.
- Make sure you write legibly.
- Make sure your meaning is clear.
- Make sure that your name is on the sheet of paper used.
- At the end of the assessment hand your resource booklet, task booklet, your answers and all notes to the supervisor.

DOCUMENT 1

WHY A WOMAN STAYS ON

Domestic violence is a difficult issue to understand. It is not just about physical and sexual abuse. It is about power and control.

Some victims feel that emotional abuse is far worse than physical abuse. The bruises heal, the broken bones mend but the long-term damage caused by emotional abuse can blight a women for life. In London a quarter of all assaults and a quarter of all murders are domestic.

Domestic violence happens regardless of class, colour or culture. Many people find it hard to understand why a woman remains in a violent relationship. But what we should be asking is what prevents a woman from leaving?

It is a hidden crime, committed behind closed doors. The reasons why a woman appears to remain with a violent partner are complicated. They feel ashamed, frightened and guilty and often blame themselves for their partner's behaviour.

Who would believe that a man who is a doctor, policeman, solicitor or judge and appears to be a warm, caring individual turns into a monster behind closed doors?

They can submit their partners to unbelievable forms of degrading and humiliating abuse, even making them eat off the floor like a dog because they are not worthy to sit at the same table as them.

A man who needs to control and possess a woman uses all types of emotional and psychological abuse ... constant criticism of what she wears, how she looks, her ability to cook, clean, be a mother or her performance in bed. Verbal abuse is common both in private and in front of others and always with the intention of putting her down.

An abuser is often careful about where he physically assaults his victim. He does not want the bruises to show, often not allowing his victim to seek medical aid, even though he has caused serious injury. Women have talked about sexual abuse stretching over years while others find it difficult to discuss it because the abuse has been so awful. Some are raped, made to commit unnatural acts or even had objects forced inside them.

Research shows that a woman is assaulted 35 times on an average before she reports it.

We need to understand something of the effect on the victim of years of abuse. They have low self-esteem, suffer from depression, feel trapped and helpless, believing that their tormentor's behaviour is their fault. Afraid to be alone, they think they cannot cope, have no control over their lives and are confused and unable to make decisions. Some take to alcohol or drugs in an attempt to block out the horror.

Some women are torn because they do not want the relationship to end – only the bad times and the abuse. At first they can't believe it has happened. They collude with him to hide it and hope he will change.

In what is known as the honeymoon period he behaves in a caring, loving way until the tensions builds up and the violence explodes again.

After an incident of abuse most women look for calm and reassurance but because they are so isolated the only one to offer comfort is the abuser. They say they are sorry, beg for forgiveness and promise it won't happen again.

But violence is always repeated and escalates both in degree and the number of incidents. When a woman believes he will kill her or the children she often makes a bid to escape.

Some women stay to preserve their husband's reputation so that his career is not ruined. Even professional women with a responsible job feel so humiliated and ashamed about what they are suffering they remain silent, unable to tell anyone, even other members of their family. Victims are often financially dependent on their abusers to the extent that they have to ask for, and justify, every penny to buy food, clothes and household essentials. He even keeps the family benefit book so she has no access to money. Consequently she has no means of escape.

Women from ethnic groups have even more barriers to cross in an attempt to get help. Asian women in particular have to deal with their culture, family, religious pressures and arranged marriages which all expect them to obey their husbands.

They may be stuck in a violent relationship and unable to speak English in order to get help. Another weapon used against them is their immigration status. They are threatened that if they attempt to get help and leave their husbands they could be deported, disgraced and humiliated or suffer further serious abuse.

Children are often used to make women stay. Men threaten that if she leaves he will take the children abroad so she will never see them again or he will put them in care. He will tell social services that she is mentally ill, alcoholic, a drug abuser or an unfit mother. Some women think they should keep the family unit together whatever the cost to themselves. A partner who occasionally abuses is better than no partner at all.

What is the alternative for a women who does leave? Low welfare benefits, no guarantee of accommodation, constant fear of her children being taken into care and always worrying that her husband will trace her and take the children away or try to kill her.

So what are we, the Metropolitan Police Service, doing? The help given to victims has been enhanced by the setting up of our domestic violence units. Domestic violence can be prevented by early intervention and our positive arrest policy, arresting abusers when there is sufficient evidence. It tells the abuser that his behaviour is not acceptable. The success of the units, a positive approach to victims and abusers and the partnership forged with other agencies in the same field has resulted in more victims coming forward. For example there was a 66 per cent increase in reported domestic violence assaults in 1991. We believe this is the tip of the iceberg. Research shows that a woman is assaulted 35 times on an average before she reports it. And it is estimated that 1 in 4 women will suffer domestic violence at some time in their lives. The officers who deal with this problem are not counsellors, their job is to let victims know the choices that are available, so they can make reasoned decisions about their situation – whether they stay and risk further violence, prosecute the abuser or leave immediately because they are at risk. They are referred on to other agencies for long-term support.

A pilot project called Domestic Violence Matters was launched in February to cover the Islington and Kings Cross areas. It is based on the work done in Ontario, Canada where trained family consultants work alongside police in the station on a shift pattern covering 18 hours a day.

Police attend the scene of the incident and if there is sufficient evidence the abuser is arrested. Then the family consultant goes to the scene and deals with the needs of the victim.

The MPS project is being funded by the Home Office and Safer Cities. It will run for three years after which it will be fully evaluated. The Met has a working party looking into domestic violence which will be producing its report soon. It has looked at all aspects of the problem including a new definition to include psychological and emotional abuse and refers to partners regardless of gender and sexual orientation.

I have talked about female victims as they are by far the majority of cases that we deal with. But we acknowledge that there are also male victims of domestic violence. And we encourage them to come forward as well.

We need to understand that as a Service and as a society victims of domestic violence need time, support, encouragement and the confidence to come to us for help.

© Metropolitan Journal
March, 1993 (Issue 5)

The extent of domestic violence

- A 1979 study in Scotland found that violence to female partners was the second most common form of assault reported to police, comprising 25% of recorded assaults (Dobash & Dobash 1979).

- 90% of women's divorce petitions using cruelty as grounds contain evidence of violence (Atkins & Hoggatt 1984).

- Between 20–30% of murder victims knew their killer as spouse, co-habitant, lover or former lover, and about 40% of all murders occur in domestic situations (Home Office).

- It has been estimated that there are ¾ million domestic violence incidents in London per year (London Strategic Policy Unit 1986).

- Violence escalates in severity and frequency over time to about 2 attacks per week per woman (Dobash & Dobash 1984).

- One in eight women have been forced to have sex by their husbands and 60% have agreed to have sex reluctantly (Painter 1990).

- A West Yorkshire study found that one third of children present during an attack tried to protect their mother, and 50% of children witnessed the abuse of their mother and/or personally experienced violence (Hanmer 1990).

- Women who have experienced domestic violence come from all walks of life. Social class, family income, level of education, and ethnic or racial background make no difference (Smith 1989).

- The Metropolitan Police receive nearly 1,500 calls per week from women suffering abuse in the home (Edwards 1986).

DOCUMENT 2

BEHIND CLOSED DOORS

One third of all violent crimes against women reported to the police are the result of domestic violence and each year at least 100 women are killed by a partner, yet domestic violence is often treated as less serious than other crimes or even as a private matter to be resolved between the individuals concerned.

In 1990 Victim Support, concerned about the number of women approaching schemes for help, set up a working party to look at the experiences of victims and to see whether the services currently available met their needs. The Inter-Agency Working Party on Domestic Violence, chaired by Mary Tuck CBE (formerly Head of Research and Planning at the Home Office), included national representatives from the Women's Aid Federation of England and Wales, Relate, the Police, the Probation Service, and social welfare, housing, legal and medical organisations.

Poor resources

The Working Party found that many women endure repeated violence in their own homes because they have no effective legal protection or realistic means of escape. Civil and criminal law on domestic violence is complex, and is often not used effectively. Many women are frightened of reporting the crime to the police or assisting with prosecution because they fear that they will put themselves and their children in greater danger. The Working Party found that in many areas there is a severe shortage of safe emergency accommodation or refuge provision.

Women may approach solicitors, GPs or housing officers to ask for help, yet the Working Party found that often these professions have no formal training in domestic violence issues. In addition there is often poor co-ordination between different helping organisations, and little information or publicity about the range of services available to women.

HRH The Princess Royal

In July this year Victim Support published the Working Party's report at a press launch in the House of Commons.

At the launch HRH The Princess Royal spoke of her concern at 'a very frightening and difficult individual problem'. Her Royal Highness commented that the report was 'a very good starting point' but added, 'it will need much greater levels of co-operation at national and local levels if the tragedy of domestic violence is to be addressed'.

The launch attracted considerable media attention.

Maintaining interest

Victim Support believes it is vitally important that strategies are developed to ensure the implementation of the report's recommendations. Victim Support is to give evidence on the report to the Home Affairs Select Committee, and is working to ensure that other Government departments give consideration to its recommendations. A national conference for professionals working with domestic violence victims is planned for the New Year.

On a local level many Victim Support schemes are considering their own services for domestic violence victims, working in close co-operation with other organisations in the community.

The report recommends that:

- A Government department should be given responsibility and resources to co-ordinate work on domestic violence.

- A national policy should be drawn up, with clear targets and a time-table for implementation.

- A multi-agency domestic violence forum should be set up locally in each area, with clear aims and objectives and adequate funding.

- All the organisations in the community which have contact with women who suffer domestic violence should improve and widen local knowledge about sources of help in order to increase access to those services.

- Offences of domestic violence should be treated with no less seriousness than crimes of violence in other contexts and the police should do all in their power to ensure the safety of the woman, both immediately and in the future.

- Additional funding should be provided for more refuges and a national telephone Helpline.

Victims Support
1991/92 Annual report

'Women who are trapped in repeated violence need emergency accommodation and other practical help before they can begin to consider long term solutions. We were aware that we could offer little practical help and that our colleagues in Women's Aid were in urgent need of additional secure funding to fulfil the vital role demanded of them. This is the first time that all the organisations which women turn to for help have worked together to seek solutions.'

Helen Reeves, Director, Victim Support

'There is a brutal but common misconception that if women do not leave, the violence they are enduring cannot be all that intolerable.
They may escape violence, but to what? To poverty, to being alone to look after the children, to live in temporary overcrowded accommodation or with relatives ... leaving friends behind, uprooting the children from school.
It takes immense courage to face this kind of indeterminate future, and the woman has to find this courage at a time when her self-esteem is being systematically undermined by personal violence against her.'

From the Inter-Agency Working Party Report on Domestic Violence

KEY SKILLS COMMUNICATION LEVEL 3 SPECIMEN PAPER: DOMESTIC VIOLENCE

Part 1 SHORT ANSWER QUESTIONS

Refer to **both** documents when answering the questions.

1. Suggest **6** reasons that the writers of the two articles suggest would prevent a women from leaving a violent relationship.

    (7 marks)

2. In your own words, explain **4** of the recommendations made in the report from the Inter Agency Working Party on Domestic Violence.

    (7 marks)

3. Summarise the actions which have been taken to address the problem of Domestic Violence.

    (7 marks)

4. Compare the effectiveness of the way information is presented in the two articles. In your answer you should comment on tone, vocabulary, style and presentational devices.

    (4 marks)

    Total 25 marks

Part 2 EXTENDED ANSWER QUESTION

Write a detailed response to the following question.

5. How important is the problem of domestic violence in our society today? Do you think enough is being done to prevent domestic violence and support its victims? You may use material from Document 1 and Document 2 to support your argument but you are asked to give your own opinion.

    (25 marks)

    Total 25 marks

MARK SCHEME FOR COMMUNICATION
LEVEL 3: DOMESTIC VIOLENCE

Part 1 Short answer section – questions 1 to 4

MARKERS PLEASE NOTE : Legibility, spelling, punctuation and grammar.
Should a candidate fail to undertake Part 2 of the paper, or produce insufficient evidence for Part 2, **use Part 1** of the paper to allocate marks for legibility, spelling, punctuation and grammar (see last section of Part 2 mark scheme for marking criteria).

Q	Spec. Code	Marking Guide	Marks
1	3.2.1	The candidate has read and selected appropriate material from **both** documents 1 and 2.	1 mark maximum.
	3.3.2	The candidate has identified a number of the following points using both documents 1 and 2: The women feel afraid, frightened or guilty. The women blame themselves. They don't want the relationship to end, only the abuse. They stay to preserve their husband's reputation. They are financially dependent on their spouse. Their culture forces them to stay. The language barrier prevents them leaving. Threat of deportation. Threats involving their children They have no effective legal protection. They don't want to involve the police because of threatened additional violence if they do. Shortage of safe emergency accommodation Poor co-ordination between emergency organisations. Little publicity about range of services.	1 mark per point made up to a maximum of 6 marks providing reference is made to both documents. **Total 7 marks**
2	3.2.1	The candidate has identified the main points from Document 2	1 mark maximum
	3.2.2	The candidate has explained **any four** of the following recommendations: A government department should be given responsibility/resources for the co-ordination of work on domestic violence. National policy drawn up with clear targets and timescale for implementation Local multi-agency domestic violence forums established Community organisations should widen local knowledge about sources of help Domestic violence offences to be treated seriously	1 mark for each point to a maximum of 5 marks

Q	Spec. Code	Marking Guide	Marks
	3.2.3	Provision of additional funding. The candidate has listed the recommendations in their own words.	1 mark **Total 7 marks**
3	3.2.1	The candidate has read and selected appropriate material from both documents.	1 mark maximum

	3.2.2	The candidate has identified the following points:
		  MPS have set up Domestic Violence Units
		  Positive arrest policy plus positive approach to victims means more are coming forward.
		  Officers inform victims of their choices and refer to other agencies for long term support.
		  Pilot project – Domestic Violence Matters
		  Working party looking into Domestic Violence
		  Victim Support have set up Interagency Working Party.
		  Maximising publicity by using HRH The Princess Royal and House of Commons
		  Evidence given to Home Affairs Select Committee
		  National Conference planned
		  Victim Support offering local services.
			1 mark for each point up to a maximum of 6 marks.
			
			Total 7 marks

4	3.2.2	Comparison of documents 1 and 2. Comparison of journalistic methods Use of quotation Use of facts and figures and a comparison of the way they are presented. Comparison of the use of bullet points Comparison of the use of subtitles Comparison of vocabulary.	Up to a maximum of 4 marks **Total 4 marks**
		TOTAL FOR PART 1	**25 MARKS**

MARK-SCHEME FOR COMMUNICATION
LEVEL 3: DOMESTIC VIOLENCE

Part 2 Extended answer section – question 5

Q	Spec. Code	Marking Guide	Marks
5	3.3.1	**PLEASE NOTE** It is acceptable for the candidate to respond in any suitable form including, for example, a letter, an e-mail, a newspaper article. The candidate has selected an appropriate style of writing in its use of: • vocabulary • sentence structure • tone.	1 + 1 + 1 to maximum of 3 marks **Total 3 marks**
	3.3.2	The candidate uses paragraphs and links information and ideas in an ordered way	2 marks maximum
	3.2.3	**Synthesis of key information** from the document and presentation of case relevant to purpose	8 marks maximum
	3.3.2	**Organisation of material** For maximum marks in the higher range, candidates must demonstrate an ability to argue logically and in depth. The argued case must include a conclusion/decision.	5 marks maximum **Total 15 marks**
	3.3.3	The text is legible. • Candidate spells, punctuates and uses rules of grammar with reasonable accuracy; she or he uses a limited range of specialist terms appropriately • Candidate spells, punctuates and uses rules of grammar with considerable accuracy: she or he uses a good range of specialist terms with facility • Candidate spells, punctuates and uses rules of grammar with almost faultless accuracy, deploying a range of grammatical constructions: she or he uses a wide range of specialist terms adeptly and with precision	1 mark 1–2 marks 3–4 marks 5–6 marks **Total 7 marks**
		TOTAL FOR PART 2	25 marks

EXEMPLAR TEST 2

LEVEL	PAPER	
Key skills – Level 3	Communication	**SEXUAL HARASSMENT**

WHAT YOU NEED:

● a resource document booklet

● this task booklet

● paper

● pens with black or blue ink.

ADDITIONAL AIDS

● dictionaries may not be used.

THERE ARE TWO PARTS TO THIS PAPER:

Part 1 – Short answer questions (25 marks)

Part 2 – Extended answer questions (25 marks)

TIME ALLOWED – 1 HOUR 30 MINUTES. THIS INCLUDES READING TIME.

To complete this activity successfully you will need to:

● read the information supplied in the task booklet and the resource booklet

● complete both parts of the paper

INSTRUCTIONS TO CANDIDATES

● Write your personal details at the top of your first sheet of paper.

● Do not open this task booklet until you are told to do so by the supervisor.

● Read each question carefully and attempt all questions.

● Write in black or blue ink only.

● Make sure you write legibly.

● Make sure your meaning is clear.

● Make sure that your name is on every sheet of paper.

● At the end of the assessment hand your resource booklet, task booklet, your answers and all notes to the supervisor.

KEY SKILLS COMMUNICATION LEVEL 3
SPECIMEN PAPER: SEXUAL HARASSMENT

Part 1 SHORT ANSWER QUESTIONS

Refer to **both** documents when answering the questions.

1. Suggest **four** actions that might be interpreted by women as inappropriate sexual behaviour.

    (5 marks)

2. Using your own words explain why innocent gestures of friendship or approval might be misinterpreted as sexual harassment.

    (7 marks)

3. Compare Jim Hodkinson's reaction to his dismissal with Deborah Tannen's examples of how men and women have reacted to an increased awareness of sexual harassment in our society. Comment also on how the writers of Document 1 and Document 2 use tone, vocabulary and style of writing to convey different attitudes towards sexual harassment.

    (10 marks)

4. In your own words, summarise the link between inappropriate sexual behaviour and power.

    (3 marks)

    Total 25 marks

Part 2 EXTENDED ANSWER QUESTION

5. Who are the true victims of sexual harassment, the women who receive unwanted sexual attention in the workplace or the men like Jim Hodkinson who lose their jobs as a result of complaints about their behaviour? You may include information from Documents 1 and 2 in your answer. You should write about 150–200 words.

    (25 marks)

    Total 25 marks

DOCUMENT 1

THE INDEPENDENT
Wednesday 10 May 2000

CLOTHES SHOPS CHIEF SACKED FOR 'GROPING' FEMALE EMPLOYEE AT AWARDS NIGHT GETS £600,000 PAY-OFF

BY TERRI JUDD AND NIGEL COPE

THE CHIEF executive of one of Britain's biggest clothing chains was sacked yesterday for groping a female member of staff at an industry dinner.

Jim Hodkinson, 56, a married man with grandchildren, was given a £600,000 pay-off to terminate his contract with the fashion company New Look, where he had been in the top job for two years. He was said to have 'touched up' one of his employees and offended another women with an inappropriate comment at the *Retail Week* awards dinner.

In what is believed to be the first time anyone of such a high position has been publicly dismissed for inappropriate sexual behaviour, New Look announced to the stock market that his dismissal was due to 'criticism of his conduct'.

After negotiations with Mr Hodkinson and his lawyers, the New Look board agreed to honour his contract, giving him a year's salary, bonus and pension as a pay-off, worth about £600,000.

Yesterday the deposed chief executive hit back, insisting: 'The incident was very, very minor and I apologised.' He said the matter has been handled appallingly, and said clashes with other board members had been the real reason behind his dismissal – a claim denied by the company chairman, Howard Dyer. A senior insider at the company said: 'If somebody touches someone in an inappropriate way and the woman feels aggrieved that is the definition in law of sexual harassment. A man cannot judge that, he is not aware of the women's feelings. There is no such thing as minor sexual harassment.'

The chief executive's 'misbehaviour' happened at a disco after the awards dinner at the Grosvenor House hotel in London on 6 March.

Mr Hodkinson was said to have 'complimented' a woman staff member on her bottom before touching it. He then made a similar comment to a young woman from a firm of head-hunters used by the company.

At the end of months of discussions and negotiations the board of New Look decided unanimously to sack Mr Hodkinson.

Mr Dyer said yesterday: 'We do not welcome this . . . and coming three weeks before our results come out, the timing for us is appalling. The last thing we wanted to do was change chief executive.'

He said the women made their separate complaints to the board within a week of the dinner and the chief executive was given his opportunity to explain. 'If it had been just a bit of tomfoolery it would have been a different set of circumstances,' Mr Dyer said.

'We took the view that this behaviour was of a serious nature, irrespective of his willingness to apologise, and could not be tolerated. He was the chief executive of a company which employs a lot of women.

'We listened to his appeal and secondly we have commitment of care to the ladies involved and did not want to drag them through the courts.'

Mr Dyer denied the real reason was a clash between the chief executive, recruited from Kingfisher in may 1998, himself and the New Look founder, Tom Singh. 'We were 100 per cent behind the chief executive,' he said.

Shares in the company have fallen recently from a peak of 245p last summer to 112.5p at yesterday's close. The new chief executive will be Stephen Sunnucks, 42, the company's retail managing director.

Speaking from his home in Dorset yesterday, with his wife of 31 years by his side, Mr Hodkinson said: 'In hindsight I shouldn't have said those things and I'm quite willing to apologise. But I feel let down, not by the company but by the board, especially the chairman who was behind all this.'

He added: 'This was at a trade dinner with 1,000 people on a packed dancefloor. Everybody was jocular and it was a good, fun evening with people enjoying themselves – you must draw your own conclusions.

'I have been paid in full for my year's contract and all the other things that go with it – that demonstrates the company is on very shaky ground.'

Mr Hodkinson's wife, Jan, described the whole affair as 'pathetic'.

DOCUMENT 2

WHAT'S SEX GOT TO DO WITH IT?

Every time we open our mouths to speak, we are taking a leap of faith – faith that what we say will be understood by our listeners more or less as we mean it. Often we are lucky, and the leap lands us safely – at least, as far as we can tell. But linguist A. L. Becker, borrowing terms from the Spanish philosopher José Ortega y Gasset, points out that everything we say, every utterance contributed to a conversation, is both exuberant and deficient. Our utterances are exuberant in the sense that others always take away meanings we did not intend or suspect, because they have associations with words and expressions that we do not have. And everything we say is deficient in the sense that others necessarily miss some of the meaning that we feel we have expressed, because we have associations with words and expressions that they do not, so we assume meanings they do not understand or suspect.

Nowhere are these ambiguities as palpable as in matters of sex, including what has come to be called sexual harassment. Just mentioning the term sets of predictable and intractable emotional reactions of anger or indignation, although these emotions may be aimed at different aspects of the phenomenon – anger at what is perceived as sexual exploitation, or at what is perceived as exploitation of the new preoccupation with it. The indeterminacy of language, the inscrutability of people's 'real' intentions, the liability of conversations we thought were about one thing coming back at us, refracted through someone else's mind, as if they were about something else entirely – all these, and the deepest and strongest currents of sexual relations and myths – muddy the waters in which women and men swim together at work.

Saying One Thing and Being Heard As Saying Another

After the second round of Clarence Thomas's confirmation hearings, when talk of sexual harassment had become ubiquitous, my dean quipped, 'That's the last time I'll kiss you hello.' He was (playfully) reflecting the concern many men have felt at that time and since: that attention to sexual harassment is putting a chill on office relations, which won't be fun anymore. Why, they wonder, do so many women want to spoil the fun? But those who are concerned with the dangers of sexual harassment are not suggesting that no friendly kisses be allowed in the office (though I have heard good arguments against kisses and hugs between faculty and students). They are simply asking that people try to be sensitive to how others respond to their behavior. The same moves that are harmless in most situations, when done in a certain way, become sources of discomfort if done in a different situation or in a different way – and of course the preferences and styles of individual others are crucial.

A young American women had a summer job as a student intern at the Latin American branch office of an American company. Although the man she worked for was nice to her and gave her a job she liked to do, she was uncomfortable working there because when he came to work in the morning, he went around the office and kissed the secretaries (all women) in greeting, including the new intern, whom he had just met. Part of what makes sexual harassment so complex is that the same symbols can have one meaning in one context or to one person and a very different meaning in another context or to another person. The same phrase or gesture can be interpreted as a show of kindness, gratitude, or love; a move in a seduction; a demand for sexual compliance; or a sign of disrespect. The young woman who didn't like her boss kissing her contrasted this bad experience with a good one involving another boss. She liked the other boss very much; he treated her with more distance and formality, which she interpreted as respect. And when that summer ended, he sent her roses to wish her luck back at school. Sending roses to a young woman could have been a gesture of romantic interest or (because any symbol that can be sent sincerely can also be faked) a move in a seduction. But in the context of their professional relationship, this woman regarded it as a welcome gesture of friendship.

Sending flowers, like any other symbolic gesture, is a cultural ritual developed over time. As sociologist Erving Goffman has pointed out, our systems of courtship and courtesy are intertwined, both based on the same "arrangement between the sexes" that our culture has developed. So it is easy for something intended as courtesy to be confused with courtship, and equally easy for the license provided by courtesy to be manipulated to phase into courtship. Furthermore, the rituals associated with men and women have developed differently, many of them growing out of the situations in which members of the genders most often met in the past: in romantic contexts. Because meeting as peers at work is relatively new, fitting the old rituals into the new context can be problematic. When regional, ethnic, and age differences are added to the ambiguity inherent in communication, the brew becomes truly daunting.

It's About Power—at All Levels

It is commonly said that sexual harassment is not about sex, but about power. I believe this is true, but the fact that it involves sex is not irrelevant. Rather, sex entails power in our culture. Most important, the corresponding statement is not always true – that sexual harassment necessarily involves the threat of reprisal from one in power toward one in a subordinate position. Although this is undoubtedly a frequent constellation, and perhaps the most frightening, it is not the whole story. Sexual harassment can be experienced at any level of power: It can be encountered among peers, and it is a frequent form of insubordination perpetrated by those of lower rank against those above them in a hierarchy.

From 'Talking from 9–5' by Deborah Tannen

MARK SCHEME FOR COMMUNICATION
LEVEL 3: SEXUAL HARASSMENT

Part 1 Short answer section – questions 1 to 4

MARKERS PLEASE NOTE : Legibility, spelling, punctuation and grammar.
Should a candidate fail to undertake Part 2 of the paper, or produce insufficient evidence for Part 2, **use Part 1** of the paper to allocate marks for legibility, spelling, punctuation and grammar (see last section of Part 2 mark scheme for marking criteria.)

Q	Spec. Code	Marking Guide	Marks
1	3.2.1	The candidate has read and selected appropriate material from **both** documents 1 and 2	1 mark maximum

	32.2.	The candidate has identified the following points using both documents 1 and 2:
		Doc 1
		    Touching inappropriately
		    Touching the woman's bottom
		    Comments on appearance.
		Doc 2
		    Inappropriate use of kissing as greeting
		    Kisses and hugs between faculty and students.
			4 marks

			Total 5 Marks
2	3.2.1	The candidate has read and selected appropriate material from **both** documents.	1 mark maximum

	3.2.2	The candidate has identified a number of the following points from both documents:
		Doc 1
		    Men are not always able to judge women's feelings accurately.
		    Actions intended as a joke may be misinterpreted.
		    Men see some behaviour simply as 'good fun'.
		Doc 2
		    The spoken word can be misunderstood.
		    Can we ever judge someone's real intentions?
		    Actions are judged differently in different contexts.
		    Personal preferences influence how an action is judged.
		    The confusion between courtesy/courtship.
			6 marks maximum

			Total 7 Marks
3	3.2.2	The candidate has identified the following points from **both** documents: Doc 1 Jim Hodkinson makes excuses for his behaviour.	*cont.*

Q	Spec. Code	Marking Guide	Marks
		He links his dismissal to personality clashes rather than inappropriate sexual behaviour. He trivialises the incident He refers to his financial rewards as if they legitimise his point of view. He transfer the responsibility for the incident to the board, saying **they** reacted badly, not him. Doc 2 High ranking University Principal makes jokes about it Men see it as a curtailment of 'office fun' Student interpreted kisses as inappropriate but welcomed flowers.	5 marks maximum
		Comparison of Documents 1 and 2 Doc 1 Use of quotations to give balanced viewpoint Link with money Use of facts and figures Reference to family relationships Use of contrasting vocabulary levels (groping/inappropriate behaviour). Doc 2 Use of subheadings Use of examples The use of elevated vocabulary Quotations from learned sources Reference to sociological terms Use of images – currents, muddy waters, brew etc.	5 marks maximum **Total 10 marks**
4	3.2.2	The candidate has identified, in their own words, the link between the two concepts and refers to both documents. Give credit for any three of the following ideas: Male bosses harass subordinate females Senior management are acting to protect women from their bosses Inappropriate behaviour can be used as a tool for dismissal Sexual harassment can be a demonstration of power Harassment can occur at any level Threats are not always used.	**Total 3 marks**
		TOTAL FOR PART 1	**25 MARKS**

MARK-SCHEME FOR COMMUNICATION
LEVEL 3: SEXUAL HARASSMENT

Part 2 Extended answer section – question 5

Q	Spec. Code	Marking Guide	Marks
5	3.3.1	**PLEASE NOTE** It is acceptable for the candidate to respond in any suitable form including, for example, a letter, an e-mail, a newspaper article. The candidate has selected an appropriate style of writing in its use of: • vocabulary • sentence structure • tone.	1 + 1 + 1 to maximum of 3 marks **Total 3 marks**
	3.3.2	The candidate uses paragraphs and links information and ideas in an ordered way.	2 marks maximum
	3.2.3	**Synthesis of key information** from the document and presentation of case relevant to purpose.	8 marks maximum
	3.3.2	**Organisation of material** For maximum marks in the higher range, candidates must demonstrate an ability to argue logically and in depth. The argued case must include a conclusion/decision.	5 marks maximum **Total 15 marks**
	3.3.3	The text is legible.	1 mark
		• Candidate spells, punctuates and uses rules of grammar with reasonable accuracy; she or he uses a limited range of specialist terms appropirately	1–2 marks
		• Candidate spells, punctuates and uses rules of grammar with considerable accuracy: she or he uses a good range of specialist terms with facility	3–4 marks
		• Candidate spells, punctuates and uses rules of grammer with almost faultless accuracy, deploying a range of grammatical constructions: she or he uses a wide range of speciliast terms adeptly and with precision.	5–6 marks **Total 7 marks**
		TOTAL FOR PART 2	**25 marks**